LION LET LOOSE

The Structure and Meaning
of St. Mark's Gospel

John Sergeant

LION LET LOOSE

THE STRUCTURE AND MEANING
OF ST. MARK'S GOSPEL

Carlisle
The Paternoster Press

British Library Cataloguing in Publication Data

Sergeant, John
Lion let loose.
1. Bible, N.T. Mark–Expositions
I. Title
226'/306

ISBN 0–85364–475–6

Photoset in Great Britain by
Photoprint, 9–11 Alexandra Lane, Torquay, Devon
and printed for The Paternoster Press,
P.O. Box 300, Carlisle, CA3 0QS
by The Guernsey Press Co. Ltd., Guernsey, Channel Islands.

CONTENTS

Forewords by Lord Blanch and Canon John Fenton   7

1. The Lion's Cage   9
2. St. Mark's Use of Dovetails   14
3. St. Mark's Use of Symbols   20
4. St. Mark's Use of Irony   28
5. St. Mark's Use of Titles   32
6. The Structure of St. Mark 1–5   42
7. The Structure of St. Mark 6:1–8:30   51
8. The Structure of St. Mark 8:31–10:45   63
9. The Structure of St. Mark 10:46–13:37   70
10. The Structure of St. Mark 14:1–16:8   76
11. Symbol and History   80

Appendix 1 St. Mark's Priority   85
Appendix 2 An Outline of St. Mark's Structure   93

FOREWORDS

This book is the product of many years of patient study of St. Mark's Gospel. It is unusual in so far as it seeks consistently to derive the message of the Gospel from the structure. It is unusual also in presenting the fruits of rigorous scholarship in a form which can be understood by any serious student of the Bible armed only with this book and the text of the Gospel.

Having myself struggled over many years to discern a convincing 'Markan outline', I have profited greatly from Mr. Sergeant's work.

LORD BLANCH

This short book on Mark's Gospel seems to me extraordinarily good; and I can see why I think it. John Sergeant and I both sat at the feet of Robert Henry Lightfoot, who taught the New Testament in Oxford before, during and after the war of 1939–1945, and anticipated much recent writing on the Gospels. Many of the points Mr. Sergeant makes are enlargements of ideas that Lightfoot suggested, and depend only on one thing else: detailed attention to the text of Mark, spread over a lifetime. Hence I find myself saying again and again as I read this book, 'Why ever did I not think of this before?'

I am very happy to recommend *Lion let Loose* to all who want a deeper understanding of this remarkable Gospel.

CANON JOHN FENTON
Christ Church Oxford.

CHAPTER ONE

THE LION'S CAGE

'I would no more think of defending the gospel than of defending a caged lion. Let it loose.' So spake the great nineteenth century preacher, Charles Haddon Spurgeon.

But the Lion of St. Mark has long been caged by the critics. Even St. Augustine called Mark a 'foot-follower and abbreviator of Matthew'.[1] From Mark's position in the Bible it would appear to be so. Quotations from St. Mark among the Church Fathers are abysmally low, compared with the other evangelists. And of the 89 gospel readings in the Book of Common Prayer, 33 are from Matthew, 27 from Luke, 24 from John, and only 5 from Mark.

150 years of modern biblical scholarship have come to the lion's rescue by showing clearly that Mark is our oldest gospel. (For Mark's priority, see Appendix 1). A closer examination of particular stories in the first two Gospels shows that it is not Mark who is the abbreviator and foot-follower of Matthew, but the other way round. The stories of Peter's mother-in-law, the Disobedient Leper, the Paralytic and his Four Friends, the Stilling of

1 Augustine: *'Pedisequus et breviator Mattaei' De Concensu Evangelistarum I, iv.*

9

the Storm, the Gadarene Swine, Jairus' Daughter, the
Murder of the Baptist, the Feeding of the Five Thousand,
the Epileptic Boy, the Blessing of the Children, and Blind
Bartimaeus, are all noticeably shorter in Matthew's
version.[2] Matthew omits some of Mark's direct speech
and historic present tenses, making the stories less
dramatic and exciting. Mark has more descriptions of the
scene, and of the emotions of Jesus and the other
characters, making his stories more vivid and poignant.

In the Stilling of the Storm only Mark tells us that the
disciples took Jesus into the ship 'just as he was',
so exhausted from his exertions that he slept in the stern
on the helmsman's cushion. Mark alone records the
presence of other ships, and the disciples' indignation:
'Carest thou not that we perish?'

In the story of Jairus' daughter it is Mark, but not
Matthew, who gives the name of the Ruler of the
Synagogue, and the full description of the woman's
illness who interrupts the journey: 'She had suffered
many things of many physicians, and had spent all that
she had, and was nothing bettered but rather grew
worse.' Mark, but not Matthew, records the disciples'
exasperation: 'Thou seest the multitude thronging thee,
and sayest thou, "Who touched me?"'. He alone notes the
second and more tragic message from the ruler's house,
and Jesus' response: 'Be not afraid, only believe.' He
alone has Jesus' command to secrecy, and the dramatic
little instance of Jesus' tender care at the very end: 'He
commanded that something should be given her to eat.'

In the Feeding of the Five Thousand Mark alone has
the description of the crowd: '. . . as sheep having no shep-

2 Compare Mark 1:29–31 reduced to Mat.8:14f.

Mark 2:1–12 to Mat.9:1–8.	Mark 1:40–45 to Mat.8:2–4.
Mark 5:1–20 to Mat.9:28–34.	Mark 4:35–41 to Mat.8:23–27.
Mark 6:14–29 to Mat.14:1–12.	Mark 5:21–43 to Mat.9:18–26.
Mark 9:14–29 to Mat.17:14–21.	Mark 6:32–44 to Mat. 14:13–21.
Mark 10:46–52 to Mat.20:29–34.	Mark 10:13–16 to Mat.19:13–15.

herd', and the disciples' indignant: 'Two hundred penny-
worth of bread is not sufficient for them!' Mark alone
describes the green grass, and the careful marshalling of
the recipients for an orderly and equitable distribution,
'. . . in one hundred ranks of fifty each, like rows of herbs
in the garden plot'.

In all such cases Mark is the great story teller, and
Matthew the abbreviator and foot-follower. No-one who
has heard Mark's little story of Jesus blessing the
children, read in the service of infant baptism, would
prefer any other version.

And yet, until very recently, Mark has still been
regarded as a foot-follower, — no longer of Matthew, but
of the Jesus traditions current before him. Mark has been
classed as a simple-minded recorder of other men's
reminiscences. So simple-minded, some say, as to record
two accounts of the same multitude feeding, the Five
Thousand and the Four Thousand. Or to include stories
to the discredit of other disciples in order to further his
own opinions on the right of Gentiles to membership of
the Church. Thus Mark's skill as an editor of the traditions has been passed over. When Mark apparently
makes a journey end at the wrong destination (6:45)
and another journey start in the wrong direction (7:31),
or when the miracles seem unaccountably to diminish
in splendour (7:32–8:26), these anomalies have been
ascribed to Mark's poor editing of the Jesus stories he
inherited. But a closer examination of Mark's structure
shows the contrary. All these seeming anomalies are
actually examples of a very careful and purposeful
editing. Mark is arranging and interpreting the Jesus
stories to disclose a gospel message, a message of special
value to the beleaguered church under Nero for which
Mark wrote.

We critics have loved to make Mark very small as an
editor in order to see over his head to the traditions
behind his writing. We have been like men in a church

looking out through a stained glass window, and so keen
to observe the scenery beyond the window that we have
missed the glorious colours and significant patterns on
the window itself. As a result, features of Mark's editing,
such as the commands to secrecy, have been shamefully
misinterpreted. We have well and truly re-caged the lion.

Lately, however, scholars have been re-discovering the
value of Mark's editing. They have discerned the colours
and patterns on the window, as it were, in various parts
of his gospel. They have been demonstrating Mark's
editorial skill in constructing a sophisticated arrangement of historical material to convey a clear gospel
message.

The time has come to put the work of these scholars
together, and discern the plan and message of the whole
book. We shall see on the stained glass window the
features of a truly magnificent 'Lion of St. Mark.' Mark is
the only evangelist who actually calls his book a 'Gospel'
(*evangelion*, Mark 1:1), and when we take him at his
word his structure and meaning become plain.

The great respect shown by both Matthew and Luke for
Mark's material makes it highly probable that he is the
John Mark of the Acts and Epistles, nephew of Barnabas,
spiritual son of Peter, and profitable fellow-labourer of
Paul.

The fact that the incident of the young man who fled
naked from the Arrest at Mark 14:51 is the only incident
which seems redundant to Mark's careful pattern, makes
it very possible that the young man is none other than
Mark himself, indicating the one occasion when he
entered personally into the story; his personal monogram
on his masterpiece. Perhaps the incident foreshadowed in
Mark's mind the nearly tragic occasion when he fled from
the work of the gospel at Perga in Pamphylia, and was
restored to fellowship only by the persistent love of his
uncle, Barnabas (Acts 13:13 and 15:36–39).

In matters of authorship and origins we are dealing

with probabilities and possibilities. But in the matter of the author's meaning and message we are looking for certainties. As we unravel Mark's seeming anomalies and Old Testament allusions and special structures, his purpose in writing and his saving message become wonderfully clear.

Note: Quotations from the Bible in this book are generally from the King James or Authorized Version. Its makers were not only superb poets; they were also exact scholars, following the originals most carefully. When modern versions try to explain as well as translate, they do not always give the best explanation. Thus the New English Bible translates the Greek word *Christos* as 'Christ' at Mark 1:1 and at Mark 14:61, (Jesus' confession), but as 'Messiah' at Mark 8:29, (Peter's confession), thereby obscuring Mark's careful construction. This is much clearer in the Authorized Version, where the Greek word *Christos* is always translated by the same English word, 'Christ'.

CHAPTER TWO

ST. MARK'S USE OF DOVETAILS

St. Mark combines fourteen of his stories into seven 'dovetails'. That is, he inserts one story into the middle of another, so that the inserted story marks the passage of time in the containing story.

When St. Matthew comes to relate the same fourteen stories he uses only four of Mark's dovetails, and St. Luke only two. Dovetailing is deliberate editorial policy in Mark, and is used not only to heighten the dramatic impact of the narrative, but also to assist the reader in the task of interpretation, as follows:

1. Mark 3:21–35

Here the Beelzebub controversy is dovetailed between the departure of Jesus' family to apprehend him as a madman, and their arrival, making a double climax to a series of conflict stories.

Mark alone records that the scribes who made the ultimate accusation, amounting to blasphemy against the Holy Spirit, came down from Jerusalem, so that the greatest of the scribes and the closest of Jesus' kin are involved together in this crucial conflict. Just as the scribes who should know best make the gravest error, so the people who should be closest to Jesus 'stand outside'.

2. Mark 5:21–43

The story of the healing of the woman with an issue of blood marks the lapse of time between the report that Jairus' daughter is seriously ill, and the report that she has died, making a double climax to a series of miracle stories.

By weaving the two stories together, Mark can show Jesus under the stress of two co-incidental crises, and portray the serenity of his confident faith. No thronging multitudes, and no seemingly conflicting demands, can disturb him. He tells the woman, 'Your faith has saved you', and Jairus, 'Only have faith.' Mark points the contrast between Jesus' serene faith and the disciples' exasperation by skilful use of the two verbs blepō, and its compound periblepō, 'look', and 'look around'. The disciples cry, blepeis ton ochlon, 'Don't you see the crowd!' But Jesus went on looking round (perieblepeto — imperfect tense), till he saw the need of the individual. The certainty of following God's will gives Jesus time for everyone even in the most adverse and trying circumstances.

Compare St. Mark's play on the two verbs didōmi and apodidōmi, 'give' and 'give back', at 12:13–17, the Question of Tribute Money. Jesus' enemies seek to impale him on the horns of a dilemma: 'Shall we give, or shall we not give?' But Jesus avoids both alternatives by the concept of giving back. Give back to the government its due share of the wealth it has enabled you to accumulate by maintaining law and order, and give back to God his due as the prime giver of all things. The notion of 'giving' to the government conceals an arrogance which does not accord with the facts. Abolish the arrogance and the dilemma disappears.

3. Mark 6:7-32

The account of the martyrdom of John the Baptist fills
the gap between the commission of the Twelve, and their
return with news of their mission. Thus the self-
condemnation of the Galilean state is linked as closely as
possible with the emergence of a faithful remnant. The
birth of a new People of God coincides with the death of
the old. Throughout this chapter, which begins with the
rejection of Jesus by his home town, Mark is explaining
why the Galilean ministry was abandoned, and a remnant withdrawn to be made into the faithful Israel of
God. Notice how the two stories intertwined at 6:7-32
explain the actions of Jesus in the two stories which
follow at 6:33-52. When Herod, his lords, high captains
and chief estates of Galilee slay the Baptist, we understand that the province rejects God's call. This rejection,
and the rejection at Nazareth which precedes it, together
constitute a double signal that Galilee will have to be
abandoned for the time being, and the Twelve withdrawn
to be made the patriarchs of a new Israel. Accordingly, at
6:45f Jesus dismisses the multitude and bids them
farewell. And at 6:47-52 as soon as the multitude have
gone he immediately gives a theophany to the Twelve
alone, the Walking on the Waters. He invites the Twelve
to become unreservedly his by confessing that he is the
Christ. There is, as we shall see, a careful theological
development all through the second gospel, which the
dovetails help us to discern and interpret.

4. Mark 11:12-21

Here the withering of the fig tree is told in two parts on
either side of the cleansing of the temple. We are shown
that although Jesus reforms the temple he knows full
well that it is doomed. The reason is that he has a much

deeper purpose, to build a temple made without hands in three days, which will be universal and permanent (14:58). To achieve this purpose he must first exercise the messianic authority given him on Palm Sunday, by turning out the traders and suffering no man to carry any vessel through the temple, even though he knows that in consequence the Only Beloved Son of God will be killed and cast out (12:8). For it is by his death that he will rend the temple veil and make the Holy of Holies accessible to Jew and Gentile (15:38f). Only on the cross can he reveal the uttermost of God's love and of man's need, and on the third day bring to light the victory which will result. This new temple will indeed be the house of prayer for all the nations, as the old temple was intended to be (11:17). The conversion of the centurion will point the way. This is the temple whose head cornerstone must be rejected by the builders if it is to be built (12:10). The Christ must reign from the tree (15:26).

By means of Mark's dovetail we begin to see that the reformation of the doomed temple, which at first sight seems ephemeral, is wise beyond our imagining. The new divinely constructed temple, where everyone can see God and come to him, can be created in no other way.

5. Mark 14:1–11

The anointing at Bethany is interposed between the plotting of the Sanhedrin to take Jesus by craft after the Passover, and the treachery of Judas, which makes possible an earlier arrest. This symbolic prologue to the Passion, the anointing of Israel's true king for burial, is dramatically presented as a picture of pure devotion and deep understanding set in a framework of black deeds. The woman's true worship shines all the brighter by being deliberately contrasted with the villainy of the chief priests and scribes and the traitor.

6. Mark 14:17–31

Here the institution of the eucharist, Christ's giving of
his very self to his own for all time, by means of bread
broken and wine outpoured, is dovetailed between the
prophecy of Judas' betrayal, and the prophecy of Peter's
denial. We are shown Christ giving himself to men in
their brokenness, men for whose bitter need nothing less
will suffice.[3]

7. Mark 14:53–72

The trial before Caiaphas is dovetailed into the story of
Peter's denials, bringing Jesus' good confession and
Peter's disowning into high relief. This dovetail and the
two before it add notably to the pathos and irony of the
Passion drama.

These seven dovetails show the great care and high
purpose exercised by the second evangelist in arranging
his material. They therefore call in question the negative
verdict which many of Mark's critics have passed on the
arrangement of the first half of his Gospel. These eight
chapters have been called by one critic 'generically
uncertain and seemingly incoherent'.[4] Another describes
them as 'lacking in both theological and biographical
articulation'.[5] For another they are 'a collection of
unstrung beads'.[6]

But what of the occasions when Jesus and his disciples
set out for Bethsaida but land at Gennesaret? Or when

3 Donald Senior C.P.: *Biblical Theological Quarterly*, Vol.13 July
1982, 67–69.
4 Frank Kermode: *Genesis of Secrecy* (Harvard 1979).
5 J.H. Cadbury: *The Making of Luke-Acts* (London 1927), 80–82.
6 K.L. Schmidt: *Der Rahmen der Geschichte Jesu* (Berlin 1919).

the appointment of the Twelve interrupts the smooth
development of the conflict stories? Or when a lesser
Messianic Banquet is recorded two chapters after the
first, and the healing miracles become more laborious? Is
it possible that Mark is not losing his grip at these points,
but signalling a message, conveying saving truth to
those with ears to hear?

The answer becomes plain if we first examine some of
Mark's other literary usages, namely his use of symbols,
his use of irony, and his use of titles.

CHAPTER THREE

ST. MARK'S USE OF SYMBOLS

The sign of the withered fig tree, which Mark places before and after the cleansing of the temple, to assist interpretation, is dropped by Luke. Instead Luke inserts his second lament of Jesus for Jerusalem, which serves the same purpose. It shows that Jesus knows the cleansing will not avail to save the temple. Instead it will lead to the creation of a new temple, made without hands, the universal worship given by God through the crucifixion. It is typical of the second and third evangelists that St. Luke should say in moving poetry what St. Mark says in vivid symbol. Mark's cryptic symbol is made plainer by Luke's substitution.

There were excellent precedents for sign language. Isaiah, the statesman-prophet, wore the dress of a slave for three years to warn his fellow-citizens of the fate awaiting them if they failed to repent. Jeremiah had his yoke, and Ezekiel his two joined staves representing Israel and Judah. Our Lord not only spoke in symbols himself; he instructed his disciples to do so. Besides the most powerful symbol of all time, bread blessed and broken and wine blessed and poured, there is the symbolic action of 'shaking off the dust under your feet'. Jesus commanded it to the Twelve at 6:11, and Paul and

Barnabas employed it at Pisidian Antioch (Acts 13:51). It was a ritual cleansing from pagan pollution on return to the Jewish homeland. Shaking off the dust therefore symbolized that the town which had refused the gospel had excluded itself from the People of God.

In St. Mark symbols are used more frequently than in the other gospels, but explained less frequently than in the other gospels. For example, both Matthew and John explain the meaning of Jesus' ride into Jerusalem on an ass's colt by quoting Zechariah 9:9. But Mark leaves it to his readers to discern the Old Testament allusion and therefore the meaning of the symbolic action.

Similarly both Matthew and John explain the significance of the parting of Jesus' garments at Calvary by quoting Psalm 22:18, but Mark affords no such assistance.

Again Mark's cryptic reference to John the Baptist as the New Elijah preparing the way for a suffering Christ by his own martyrdom (9:11–13) is clearly explained by Matthew 17:13: 'Then the disciples understood that he spake unto them of John the Baptist'.

Again Mark's mysterious reference to the building of a new temple for the true worship of God by the passion and resurrection is clearly explained by John 2:21: 'He spake of the temple of his body'.

But why does Mark leave unexplained symbols and scriptural allusions which later evangelists uncover? For one thing, Mark writes for a more limited audience. Mark's is a very personal Gospel, written for people to whom Alexander and Rufus, the sons of Simon of Cyrene, and James the Little and Joses, the sons of Mary, needed no introduction.[7] He writes for Church members who possessed means of interpreting his signs and dark sayings which were not available to 'those outside'. Three

7 J.C. Fenton: 'The Mother of Jesus in Mark's Gospel and its Revisions' *Theology* Vol. 86 1985, 433–437.

times, at 4:10–20, at 4:32f, and at 7:17–23, Mark says that Jesus spoke to the multitude in mysterious parables, and expounded them afterwards to his disciples 'privately', 'in the house', 'away from the crowd'. Mark is telling his readers that 'knowing the mystery of the Kingdom of God' is a gift, and that this gift is available in the Church, where the Risen Christ still interprets the scriptures and the memoirs of the apostles through his appointed prophets and teachers. It is hardly surprising therefore that later evangelists, writing for wider audiences, should find it advisable to explain some of Mark's more esoteric symbols, and omit some of his subtler constructions.

The Greek word *parabolē* means 'thrown alongside'. Mark uses it to denote anything from a simple simile to a full length allegory which is thrown alongside a doctrine by way of illustration. The illustrations which Mark calls parables at 3:23–27, the Divided House, the Divided Kingdom, and the Strong Man's Goods, need no interpreting. Nor do those he calls parables at 12:1–12, the Wicked Husbandmen and the Chief Cornerstone. These five parables are all given in the cut and thrust of controversy, and their meaning is immediately clear to friends and foes alike.

On the other hand the five parables at 4:1–34 are not clear even to Jesus' closest disciples. These five are thrown alongside 'the mystery of the Kingdom of God', the paradox of joy attained by suffering and power by self-abasement, the mystery of spiritual life made available for man by the death of the Son of Man. Interpretation here is a gift of God (4:11). It is given when Jesus' disciples meet with him privately and ask him, just as they met with Christ after the Resurrection in prayer to him in the fellowship of his church. Similarly the mysterious parable of Defilement from Within, 7:14–16, is given to all, but its meaning only to the few. Jesus cries, 'Hearken unto me everyone of you, and understand.' But the only ones to find the solution are those who meet with Jesus in the house and ask him for enlightenment.

In chapters four and seven therefore Mark has selected parables which need interpreting, and has seized the oppportunity to show his readers where interpretation is to be found — in the inspired community.

As with the parables, so it is with the symbols which are dramatized parables. Some, like the child in the midst (9:36f), are immediately clear to all. Others, like the ass's colt, are explained by later evangelists. Others are mysterious. Expositors differ. Fortunately Mark gives us precious clues to the meaning he himself attaches to the mysterious symbols by the context in which he places them, either in his dovetails or in his unfolding drama of revelation and response. Thus the meaning of the withered fig tree is disclosed by its dovetailing with the cleansing of the temple. And the meaning of the rent temple veil is disclosed by its position in the drama. Mark's drama is a desperate duel of light and darkness, leading to two crucial victories for the light, St. Peter's confession at 8:29 and the centurion's confession at 15:39. At the apex of the whole drama, as soon as Jesus has paid the full price of our ransom and died upon the cross, two short verses, 15:38, 39, show what the Passion has achieved. At 15:38 the veil of the temple is torn in two from the top. The Holy of Holies is opened, not just once a year on the Day of Atonement, and not just for the High Priest alone to enter, but for all believers. As the next verse shows, even the centurion, the first-fruits of the Gentiles, can now see the truth. The rent veil means that anyone who confronts Calvary and there takes the measure of God's love for him, and of his need for God, can have the conversion experience, can enter into life and become a subject of the Kingdom of God. Because the veil is torn from the top, we understand that it is rent by the hand of God. God makes the innermost sanctum freely available by the blood of Christ. Mark's word for veil, *katapetasma*, is used in the Septuagint (Greek) translation of Exodus 26:33: 'The veil shall make a separation between the holy place and the Holy of Holies.' Hebrews 10:19–22 was written to Christians who understood the connection between the torn veil of the temple and the torn flesh of the crucified Christ, and that entry into the sanctuary was made possible by Christ's sacrifice.[8]

The symbolic significance of the miracles of sight is also indicated by their context. There are only two healings of the blind in Mark. The first, the blind man of Bethsaida, introduces the gift of spiritual sight to Peter and the Twelve. The second, blind Bartimaeus, introduces the gift of spiritual sight to the demonstrating multitude on Palm Sunday. The miraculous gift of physical sight in Mark signals that God's grace is about to bestow the far greater gift of spiritual sight.

Other problems in Mark's Gospel may be resolved when his language of symbols is understood. Jesus' promise at 14:28, 'After I am risen I will go before you into Galilee', confirmed by the angel at the sepulchre with the added words, 'There shall ye see him' at 16:7, has been variously interpreted as an attempt to reconcile Galilean and Judean traditions of the Easter appearances, or alternatively as summoning pilgrims to the place of Jesus' Parousia. But Galilee in Mark's Gospel is the location of Jesus' recorded minstry, a ministry shared with the Twelve, a ministry left for a call to Jerusalem which has now been accomplished. 'Going before into Galilee' could therefore mean that the Risen Christ will resume his mission in Galilee through his Church. The disciples are bidden to return to the hungry multitudes with the words of life, and the Easter experience will be

8 Harry L. Chronis: *Journal of Biblical Literature* March 1982, 101–103.

theirs. Following Christ into Galilee could mean, in Mark's symbolic language, undertaking Christ's work under Christ's direction, and thereby experiencing Christ's presence — an experience to which all his saints can testify.[9]

If Mark sometimes wraps up his good news in mysterious parables and symbols and scriptural allusions, that may be an appropriate packaging for the special circumstances for which Mark wrote. Up to the year 67 AD the Church made phenomenal progress throughout the Roman world. Already she could have uttered Tertullian's proud boast: 'We are but of yesterday, and we have filled all you possess.' When St. Paul was acquitted at his first trial before Nero, and he and Peter worked together in Rome, all their differences at Antioch composed, hopes ran high that the response of the Roman world to the gospel would be positive. Then tragedy struck. Nero was building his incredible luxury palace, the *Domus Aurea*, on the ruins of the Great Fire of Rome, and was everywhere accused of starting the fire for his own purposes. So Nero found a scapegoat in the infant Church. Most probably in the same year that he dispatched Vespasian with overwhelming forces to destroy the Holy City and temple and Jewish homeland, he slew Peter and Paul in Rome, with 'a great multitude of the elect'.[10] Christians were suddenly being deprived of their greatest leaders in Rome and their deepest roots in Jerusalem, and finding themselves exposed to the full fury of every conscience wounded by the gospel challenge. So Mark retells the life and Passion and Resurrection of Jesus in such a way as to illumine for the Church the black and bitter tragedies of AD65–70.

---

9 'In pursuit of its mission, the community would come to see and understand the meaning of its discipleship.' Donald Senior: *The Passion of Jesus in the Gospel of Mark* (Chicago 1984), 136.
10 The First Epistle of Clement 5:6f.

A dark cloud of tragedy hangs over the whole of Mark's Gospel. The Galilean ministry (1:1–8:30) is portrayed as a forecast and interpretation of the Passion. The next section, the journey to Jerusalem (8:31–10:45) is built around the three predictions of the Passion, and Christ's teaching on the *via crucis* which each of these predictions introduces. The Passion itself is sombre till the very end, with none of the brilliant flashes of heroism and compassion added by Luke and John, nor the extra miracles of Matthew. The only word heard from the cross is the cry of dereliction.

Mark alone adds to the list of earthly blessings of the faithful at 10:30 the words 'with persecutions'.

John the Baptist has only four mentions after he has baptized Jesus, and three of them are tragic. First, his imprisonment at 1:14. Second, a long and vivid account of his martyrdom at 6:14–29. Third, an explanation of his role as the martyred forerunner of a martyred Messiah at 9:11–15.

The doctrine of the cross was already there for Mark to use in the Church's sudden crisis of faith. It was eloquently expounded in Paul's epistles to the Corinthians and Romans, written before Mark's Gospel. Rather it is the extra sombreness of Mark's Passion story, and the tragic tone apparent all through the rest of his gospel and not repeated by later evangelists, which point to the horrors of Nero's persecution.

Mark shows his readers that the blackest of tragedies can still be good news: for it is when Jesus pays the full price that he rends the temple veil and opens the Kingdom of God to all believers (15:37–39). Mark is calling Christians to interpret their pains by Jesus, and to see them as the means of both gaining heaven and saving the world. He writes for a church confronted by dark mysteries: 'Why should the world turn with such ferocity and suddenness against those who bring the world good news?' 'Why should tyrants be allowed to get away with such appalling cruelty and mendacity?' Such baffling tragedies could be explained only within the spirit-filled community, and Mark directs his readers thither. He knows his parables and symbols and scriptural allusions will be rightly interpreted within the church, where alone the mystery of the Kingdom of God is made known, and the doctrine of the saving cross is preached. Arcane language may be inappropriate for outsiders seeking information. It is not inappropriate for teachers of the initiated faced with baffling mysteries.

CHAPTER FOUR

ST. MARK'S USE OF IRONY

At Mark 3:4 Jesus asks his critics: 'Is it lawful to do good on the sabbath days, or to do evil? To save life, or to kill?'

The bitter irony of these words appears shortly, at 3:6, when the critics take counsel with their political opponents 'how they might destroy him.' Because Jesus heals a withered hand on the Sabbath, the Pharisees are so outraged that they themselves commit the worst possible profanation of the holy day, the plotting of murder.

A similar delayed action irony appears at 14:1–11, when Jesus' foes are pressing in on him, and the end is near. A woman shows that she at least owns Jesus as her sovereign by anointing his head with costly perfume. 'She has come beforehand' says Jesus, 'to anoint my body for burial'. The dramatic irony of these words is not revealed until 15:43–16:6, when Jesus' body is buried in haste before the sabbath begins, and the women come as soon as the sabbath ends to make good the anointing with aromatic oils, only to find that they have arrived too late. The body has gone. The prophetic understanding of the woman with the pure oil of nard is so wonderful that her story is to be told wherever the gospel is proclaimed in all the world.

There is a double irony in Peter's response to the

Transfiguration at 9:5: 'Rabbi, it is good for us to be here, and let us make three tabernacles, one for thee, and one for Moses, and one for Elijah.' Peter's offer of tabernacles underlines the reality and objectivity of the vision. The irony is that by his use of the two words 'three' and 'tabernacles', Peter shows that he has doubly misinterpreted the vision. Peter's fear and confusion are immediately answered, when Moses, the giver of the law, and Elijah, the father of the prophets, are faded out, leaving Jesus only, and the Divine Voice proclaims: 'This is my only beloved Son. Hear him.' Hitherto God's people have had two guides to life, the Law and the Prophets. 'The Law and the Prophets were until John, and since that time the Kingdom of God is preached' (Luke 16:16). Mark 10: 1–12 shows how Moses the Lawgiver and Malachi the Prophet appear to differ on the subject of divorce. Moses states what the Law allows, and Malachi what the Deity desires.

The Transfiguration proclaims that henceforth God's people have one light, the One in whom both the Law and the Prophets find fulfilment. Only when the Law and the Prophets talk with Jesus, and then leave him in sole possession of the field, will God's will be done on earth as it is in heaven. The very moment when heaven reveals that there is one sole light for mankind is chosen by Peter to propose three tabernacles!

But not only does Peter's call for three tabernacles contradict a vision of oneness: the whole idea of tabernacling on the mountain is completely mistimed. For down in the valley the other nine disciples are being totally defeated by an evil spirit, and the whole multitude is in confusion. God's call is not to tabernacle on the mount, but to engage in fierce combat in the valley. The supreme enthronement of Jesus, shown to the three on the heights, must now be demonstrated to the multitude below, by victory over the most powerful and deadly of the demons.

Peter's misunderstanding is total.

Another irony of double error is shown by the by-standers at Golgotha. They mistake Jesus' loud 'cry of dereliction' for a call to Elijah to come and save him. The irony is that as Jesus has already explained to the three disciples at 9:11–13, and as St. Mark's readers already know, Elijah has come and gone already. For Jesus' Elijah is none other than John the Baptist, who has suffered martyrdom, and has thus fittingly prepared the way for a Christ who saves by suffering. The prophet they think Jesus is calling to the rescue is known by Jesus to have 'come already', and to have shown the way to the redemptive suffering which they now blindly witness. Jesus saves precisely because he is not rescued.

At the same time the bystanders offer Jesus the wine he has renounced at the Last Supper, 'until that day when I drink it new in the Kingdom of God', the very drink he deliberately refused before crucifixion. Altogether mis-understanding reaches its nadir in this darkest hour before the full price is paid, and the full splendour of love revealed, and believers are ransomed.[11]

There is bitter irony also in the two false accusations underlined at the Jewish and Roman trials respectively.

At the Jewish trial the allegation is: 'We heard him say, "I will destroy this temple made with hands, and within three days I will build another made without hands".' The irony is that Jesus' foes are achieving the very thing they accuse him of. They are enabling him to build in three days, by his Passion and Resurrection, a temple where Jew and Gentile have access to the mercy seat.

At the Roman trial he is accused of making himself king of the Jews. The irony here is that Pilate and his soldiers, by their crown of thorns, by their mock obeis-

11 Kent Brower: 'Elijah in the Markan Passion Narratives' *Journal for the Study of the New Testament*, Issue 8, June 1983, 85–101.

ance, by their derisory *titulus*, are enthroning Jesus in the hearts of believers. They are actually making him what they deride him for trying to make himself. What they think is a mock enthronement is in fact the most real and lasting enthronement history has known.

At Golgotha the passers-by deride Jesus with the false accusation made at the Jewish trial. 'Ah, thou that destroyest the temple, and buildest it in three days . . .' (15:29). And the chief priests echo the false accusation at the Roman trial. 'Let the Christ, the King of Israel, descend now from the cross . . .' (15:32). The dramatic ironies of both false accusations are thus brought together at the climax of the drama.

Elsewhere the sharp edge of Mark's irony may have been blunted by translators who did not believe that Mark was capable of anything quite so sophisticated. The single Greek word *ochlos* is translated 'multitude' or 'people' or 'press' in the Authorized Version, and as 'crowd' or 'people' or 'mob' in the New English Bible. But St. Mark, by using the same word throughout, indicates that the entourage of eager admirers, who have been the object of Jesus' compassion all through his ministry, are the very same type of people who, at the final crisis, are moved by the chief priests to prefer Barabbas, and procure the sentence of crucifixion by their loud insistence. The bitter irony of 15:11 — 'The chief priests stirred up the *ochlos*' — and of 15:15 — 'Pilate, wishing to content the *ochlos*' — is lost in our translations.

But Mark's original readers also had their entourage of inquirers and admirers, who, because they were not fully committed, were apt to turn traitor under the ferocity of the Neronian persecution. Christians in Mark's day would be quick to appreciate his irony, and would be strengthened to know that the bitterest betrayal had been endured and overcome by the Author and Perfecter of their faith.

CHAPTER FIVE

ST. MARK'S USE OF TITLES

Jesus' question, 'Whom say ye that I am?' has nine distinct answers in Mark's Gospel. Nine different titles disclose the secret identity of Jesus of Nazareth, which is Mark's recurrent theme. Why nine? Only one of the titles is said to be of less value than the others. This is the title 'Son of David', used by Bartimaeus at the ascent to Calvary's throne (10:47f). At 12:33–37 Jesus points out that the Christ is much more than Son of David, seeing that David in Psalm 110 calls him Lord. Yet even this inadequate appellation, Son of David, was enough to give Jesus the messianic authority to turn the traders out of the temple, and to take control there, allowing no man to carry any vessel through the sacred precincts. The Son of David title, recalling past national greatness, was perhaps the title most nearly associated with a violent solution for the nation's problems as distinct from the moral and spiritual solution preached by Jesus.

The other titles cannot have differing values because they are used interchangeably. For instance, four of the titles are used together at the pivot of the drama, (14:61f). When the High Priest asks Jesus, 'Are you the Christ, the Son of the Blessed One?', he uses two of the titles. And when Jesus answers, 'I am, and you will see the Son of Man . . .', he uses two more.

When Peter confesses at 8:29 that the rejected Jesus is the Christ, and when the centurion at 15:39 declares that the crucified Jesus was the Son of God, they are not saying two things about Jesus. They are saying the same thing, each in his own language. The secret identity of Jesus is always the same. Mark always portrays him as the human reviled and persecuted to the uttermost, proved by the uttermost testing and found true; able therefore to reveal the uttermost of God's love and command our uttermost allegiance; able therefore to bestow eternal life, and admit to the Kingdom of God. This one secret is expressed in nine different ways, each appropriate for the speaker. The Jewish title *Ho Christos*, the Anointed, taken from the Jewish scriptures, is appropriate for Peter, the first Jew to discern the secret. The Gentile equivalent, Son of God, is appropriate for the centurion at Golgotha, who is portrayed by Mark as the firstfruits of the Gentiles.

Similarly, the title Son of the Blessed One, with its deferential circumlocution for the Deity, is appropriate for the High Priest. Matthew uses a similar substitute for the word God when he changes Mark's phrase 'Kingdom of God' into 'Kingdom of Heaven'.

Similarly the title My Only Beloved Son, *Ho huios mou ho agapētos*, is appropriate for God the Father, and the title I AM, *Egō Eimi*, is appropriate for Jesus to use of himself.

Four of the nine titles are technical theological terms, and need briefly explaining. They are: *Ho Christos*, the Anointed; *Ho Agapētos*, the Only Beloved; *Egō Eimi*, I AM; and *Ho Huios tou Anthrōpou*, the Son of Man. Fortunately a clear explanation of all four technical terms is given in the Old Testament, or rather in the Greek translation of the Old Testament known as the Septuagint, or Version of the Seventy, made in Alexandria around 200 BC and used regularly in the churches for which Mark wrote.

The phrase translated 'The Anointed' in our English versions of 1 and 2 Samuel, 1 and 2 Chronicles, and some of the Prophets and Psalms, is invariably rendered *Ho Christos* in the Septuagint. In 1 Samuel David has power to slay the lion and the bear and the giant, and to drive out the demon from King Saul with his music, because he has received the Spirit of God through Samuel's private anointing. Armed with this Spirit, David can face rejection and exile, and go on to become the nation's deliverer. So in Mark's Gospel the promised deliverer is enabled to conquer the demons of sickness and deformity and madness, of tempest and hunger, because the Spirit of God has descended upon him at his baptism. Like David's superhuman exploits, the miracles of Jesus are the outward manifestation of spiritual anointing. In Mark's Gospel the Descent of the Dove at Jesus' baptism, and the call to be God's Only Beloved Son in whom he is well pleased, are revealed to Jesus only. None but the demons, supernatural beings, can see Jesus's divine identity, until Peter, after much groping in the dark, at length perceives the meaning of the miracles when he confesses: 'You are the Anointed.'

Confusion arises because the infant Church, very early in its life, dropped the article from the *ho Christos* title. Jesus the Anointed became Jesus Anointed. The title became the surname. 'Jesus Christ', used as forename plus surname, without the article, occurs 132 times in Paul's epistles, twice in Matthew's Gospel, twice in John's, and seventeen times in the Acts. So when St. Mark starts his book: 'The beginning of the gospel of Jesus Christ . . .' he is using Christ without the article as a surname, just as Paul does, and the other three evangelists. But four times thereafter Mark uses *ho Christos* with the article, as a title.[12]

---

12 At Mark 8:29, 13:21, 14:61 and 15:32. The genitive at 9:41 is a different case.

Peter's confession at 8:29: 'You are *the* Anointed' gives Jesus absolute allegiance so far as the disciples conceive it. But Jesus immediately tells them how much more is involved in being The Anointed than they have yet imagined. And he goes on to explain to the disciples, with the people (*ochlos*), the quality of allegiance he requires (8:31–38).

Ho Christos is used again with the article as a title at 14:61, when the High Priest asks Jesus: 'Are you *the* Anointed, the Son of the Blessed One?' By his positive reply Jesus gives himself to the cross for our redemption. So the title *ho Christos*, given at 8:29, and accepted at 14:62, explains the surname at 1:1, and shows how this surname was earned.

The Old Testament background for the title 'My Only Beloved Son' is Genesis 22, the story of Abraham's offering of his one and only legitimate son and heir in sacrifice. The phrase '*ton huion sou ton agapētos*' occurs three times in the Septuagint version of this chapter. Abraham's sacrifice is total because Isaac is his only remaining child, and the only hope of founding the race of God's appointing, for which Abraham has sacrificed everything at God's call. *Agapētos* carries the sense 'best beloved because unique', 'the one and only'. Aristotle cites the case of a plaintiff requiring extra damages for the loss of an eye because it was his *agapētos* eye.[13]

The *agapētos* title occurs three times in Mark. At 1:11 it is spoken to Jesus only at his baptism. At 9:7 it is spoken to the three chosen disciples at the Transfiguration. And at 12:6 it is allocated by Jesus to himself, with great dramatic effect, in the parable of the Wicked Husbandmen. 'Having yet therefore one son, his well-beloved, (*agapētos*), he sent him also last unto them, saying "They will reverence my son". But those husband-

13 H.B. Swete: *The Gospel According to St. Mark* (London 1909), 10[3].

men said among themselves: "This is the heir; come, let us kill him . . .".

The title *Ego Eimi*, I AM, is also used three times in St. Mark. It is used by Jesus to disclose his identity to the Twelve when he walks on the waters, claiming their recognition after the Feeding of the Five Thousand, at 6:50. It is used by Jesus again at 14:62, where he is confessing his true identity before the High Priest and full council.

Meanwhile Jesus uses it again at 13:6 to describe the false claims of pseudo-Christs: 'Many shall come in my name, saying that I AM'. Here again the Septuagint, or Greek Old Testament, gives the meaning of the title, and explains its double use. In Deutero-Isaiah, the prophet of the exile, the title I AM is used eight times for God's self-disclosure, suggesting his eternity and infinity and sole sovereign might, and twice for Babylon's false claim to divine might.[14]

The numinous quality of the I AM proclamation is shown by St. John, at the climax of Jesus' dispute with the Pharisees 'Before Abraham was, I AM' (John 8:58). And again at the Arrest (John 18:4–9), where Jesus' declaration 'I AM' causes the band of armed men and officers from the chief priests to go backward and fall to the ground. The same phrase 'I AM' is used at John 8:28 and 13:19.

The title which Jesus uses when teaching his disciples the need for his Passion and Resurrection to ransom believers is 'Son of Man'. In the Septuagint *'ho huios tou anthrōpou'* ordinarily means man in his frailty and transitoriness, as contrasted with the permanence of God and his angels. The phrase is so used in the Greek Old Testament at Numbers 23:19, Job 25:6, Job 35:8, in Psalms 8, 80, 144 and 146, and in the prophets Isaiah, Jeremiah, and Ezekiel, 104 times in all. 'Who art thou',

14 At Isaiah 43:10, 43:25, 46:4, 47:8, 47:10, 48:12 and 51:12.

asks Isaiah, 'that thou shouldst be afraid of a man that shall die, and of the son of man that shall be made as grass' (Isaiah 51:12)?

But just once in the Old Testament 'son of man' has a special sense. In Daniel 7 the son of man represents the saints of the Most High. Here he is no longer contrasted with the sons of God, above him, who all shouted for joy when the world of men was created (Job 38:7). Instead he is contrasted with the creatures beneath him, the winged lion, the bear, the leopard, and the dreadful and terrible beast, representing the Assyrian, Babylonian, Persian, and Greek empires. This son of man comes with the clouds of heaven to the Ancient of Days, and receives a kingdom which, unlike the bestial empires, is universal and permanent (Daniel 7:1–14).

The term 'son of man' therefore had a dual connotation in the Old Testament. It could signify either man in his feebleness, or man exalted above all, and given the task initiating the kingdom of God on earth. Hence the title was specially apt when Jesus taught his disciples about his own destiny. It claimed so little but suggested so much. Jesus was prophesying that the Son of Man must undergo the utmost humiliation, betrayal and suffering, and thereby come to Resurrection and world dominion, as the man destined to bring the reign of God on earth as it is in heaven.

But when the crunch comes, when Jesus is asked to identify himself before the High Priest and whole Council, all doubt as to the meaning of the phrase Son of Man is removed. The title is given its full apocalyptic connotation by the two quotations which follow it: '. . . sitting on the right hand of power', from the messianic Psalm 110, and '. . . coming with the clouds of heaven', from Daniel 7. In Mark's account Jesus replies to the High Priest's question with the resounding affirmative which seals his fate and saves the world: 'I AM, and you will see the Son of Man . . .'

In the second gospel the Son of Man title occurs only on the lips of Jesus, and only after Peter's confession, with two exceptions. These are 2:10, ('So that you may see that the Son of Man has power on earth to forgive sins') and 2:28 ('Consequently the Son of Man is lord even over the sabbath'). Both occur within a series of conflict stories carefully arranged to show the ever-widening gulf between the real religion of Jesus and the sham religiosity of his opponents. But by their very nature conflict stories have incidental lessons to teach, and here Mark has included two such lessons of special value to the early Church. 2:10 teaches that the risen Christ has authority in his Church to forgive sins (e.g. to re-admit lapsed but penitent Christians). And 2:28 teaches that the risen Christ in his church has authority to re-order sabbath worship (e.g. to honour the first day of the week instead of the seventh). A modern author would put such *obiter dicta* in a bracket or a footnote. Indeed St. Mark's Greek reads much better if these two 'Son of Man' sayings are understood parenthetically.

The use of conflict stories to teach incidental lessons in Mark can be better understood by referring to 7:19, where the same phenomenon recurs. Here controversy returns when the disciples have failed to comprehend the Feeding of the Five Thousand, and repetition of all aspects of Jesus' ministry is necessary for their sakes. Again there is controversy. And again Mark inserts into a conflict story an *obiter dictum* of great moment for the church of his day, '. . . cleansing all meats'. Jewish Christians can have table fellowship with Gentiles who do not observe the Mosaic food laws.

Each of these seven titles therefore, 'The Christ', 'The Son of God', 'My Only Beloved Son', 'I AM', 'The Son of Man', 'The Son of David', and 'The Son of the Blessed One', are appropriate for the speaker and context. The other two titles are bestowed by devils. The unclean spirit in the synagogue at 1:24 calls Jesus 'The Holy One

of God'. And the Gadarene demoniac at 5:7 hails him as
'Son of God Most High'. The unclean bows to the holy,
and the uncontrollable to the incarnation of divine
supremacy. The devils in the summarizing section, 3:11,
use the same title as the centurion at the cross, 'Son of
God'. St. Mark in fact makes it plain that the devils'
insight was not mistaken, but that its publication was
premature before the Passion, and they were silenced for
this reason.[15]

According to the received text, Mark proclaims two of
these nine titles in his opening verse: 'The beginning of
the gospel of Jesus Christ Son of God'. These two titles,
'Christ' and 'Son of God', outline Mark's master theme,
for the first half of his book leads up to a climax in Peter's
confession that Jesus is the Christ, and the second half to
a climax in the centurion's confession that he is Son of
God. The difficulty is that the words 'Son of God' at 1:1
are missing from a minority of ancient manuscripts.[16]
But fortunately 1:1 is not the only place where Mark
discloses his master theme. He does so also at the pivotal
verse 14:61. The High Priest's question, when due
allowance is made for high-priestly language, becomes:
'Are you the Christ, the Son of God?' Therefore, whether
the words Son of God at 1:1 are original or not, it is still
plain that Mark has a master theme based on the two
titles 'Christ' and 'Son of God'. The first eight chapters
show the price Jesus paid to win from Peter the Jewish
title, 'The Christ', and the next seven the price he paid to
win from the Gentile centurion the title 'Son of God'.

These two titles, 'Christ' and 'Son of God', occur
together again at John 20:31, the last verse before his
postscript, a verse which sums up in a remarkable way,
whether intentionally or not, both the theme and purpose
of St. Mark: 'These are written that ye might believe that

15 See below on Mark's twin secrecy motifs, pages 58–61.
16 C.E.B. Cranfield: *St. Mark* (Cambridge 1959), 38.

Jesus is the Christ, the Son of God, and that believing ye
might have life through his name.'

The use of nine different titles for Jesus adds to the
mystique of Mark's Gospel. It also makes room for the
interpretation which was available only within the
Church. St. Mark would have been plainer if he had used
fewer titles. Plainer too if he had inserted the articles at
1:1, and written: 'The Christ, The Son of God', as at John
11:27 and at John 20:31. But Mark does not claim that
his Gospel is plain to everyone. He explains in his
parable chapter that his message is a mystery which is
revealed by God to those who live the life of faith and
belong to the community of faith. We need the interpretation which Jesus gave to his disciples in private, and
still gives in his Church. It is no accident that two of the
titles have double meanings. *Egō eimi* can mean 'I am', =
'It's me', or 'I AM', = 'Eternal God'. *Huios tou anthrōpou*
can mean 'son of man', = 'merely human', or 'Son of
Man', = 'Divine Saviour'. The use of enigmatic titles
invites the work of the Church's prophetic interpreters,
spokesmen of the risen Christ.

In his titles, as in his parables, Mark employs the
language of mystery for a darkly mysterious period in
the Church's history, when the identity of Jesus of
Nazareth was still a dreadul but life-giving secret. It was
dreadful because confessing Jesus to be the Christ meant
so much more, in 67 AD, than a polite bow to a prevailing
orthodoxy. It meant identification with a tiny minority of
God-filled people who had undermined the conscience of a
slave-owning, self-indulgent society, and brought down
upon themselves hatred and calumny and persecution
(Mark 13). It was life-giving because confessing Jesus,
crucified by men, to be Son of God, meant being 'crucified
unto the world'. It meant a liberation of the soul from all
worldly values, a self-emptying and God-filling. It meant
being set free to enter the Kingdom of God as defined by
St. Paul at Romans 14:17: 'The Kingdom of God is . . .

righteousness and peace and joy in the Holy Ghost' — a present experience with future consequences.

But confessing Jesus to be the Son of God before his Passion would not have had the same doctrinal and moral implications. In Mark's Gospel only the devils wished to reveal Jesus' identity before his Passion.

CHAPTER SIX

THE STRUCTURE OF ST. MARK 1–5

St. Mark's careful editing of his historical material has been shown in his use of dovetails, symbolism, irony and varied titles for Jesus. We are now in a position to examine each section of his gospel in turn, and see whether the same careful editing persists.

Mark begins with an historical prologue, which has echoes in the philosophical prologue of St. John. Then he plunges straight into a description of the Galilean ministry. He uses the literary device of first giving a comprehensive account of twenty-four hours in one town, and then recording that Jesus 'went on to the next towns throughout all Galilee'.

In only nineteen verses, 1:21–39, he conveys vividly the shattering effect upon Capernaum of a life filled with divine wisdom and power, as described in the prologue. It is a life crammed with activity, and yet giving priority to prayer in solitude. Mark records the successive reactions of Capernaum's citizens to swiftly moving events. First astonishment, *exeplēssonto*; they are thunderstruck when Jesus teaches with authority. Then amazement, *ethambēthēsan*; they are awestruck when he vindicates that authority by casting out an unclean spirit. Only the demon, a supernatural being, knows the reason for such authority and power, namely that Jesus is 'the Holy One of God'.

After the public epiphany in the synagogue comes the private healing in the house. Simon's wife's mother is immediately cured and 'ministers unto them'. Even the lunch hour interval in this specimen day is filled with miracle. And at sundown, when the sabbath ends, and all the sick can be brought, he ministers to 'all the city'.

But even this is not the climax. The next astonishing event reveals the secret of Jesus' power. He rises a great while before day to pray in a solitary place. The disciples, who have made no such sacrifice for prayer, try to drag Jesus down to the level of what all men expect of him. By contrast, the man of prayer has seen past what men expect to the perfect will of God. 'Therefore came I forth' has a double meaning. It can mean 'Therefore came I forth from Capernaum this morning', or 'Therefore came I forth from God'.

Mark employs the adverb *euthus*, immediately, nine times in the twenty-one verses 1:10–30, to express the hurricane impact of the gospel.

In this specimen day the authoritative teaching comes first, and the miracle which vindicates it second. And Mark goes on to give a fuller account, first of Jesus' teaching, 4:1–34, and then of the miracles which authenticate the teaching, 4:35–5:34. However, since the teaching in chapter four is given in parables, which not only enlighten the responsive but also judge the recalcitrant, Mark prefaces his teaching section with a section on the rise of opposition. So the first five sections of St. Mark follow a logical and historical sequence:

(1) The prologue (1:1–20)
(2) A typical day (1:21–39)
(3) The rise of opposition (1:40–3:35)
(4) The parables (4:1–34)
(5) The miracles (4:35–5:43)

But there is a difficulty. Whereas the other four
sections contain no disparate material, the conflict
stories have a preface and an interlude, the Disobedient
Leper (1:40–45) and the Appointment of the Twelve
(3:13–19), which at first sight do not seem to belong.
These require an explanation.

Mark 1:40–3:35

The seven conflict stories are arranged to show step by
step the development of hostility to the gospel which the
words and deeds of Jesus proclaim. They begin with a
story of unspoken resentment (2:1–12). Jesus asks the
scribes, 'Why do you question thus in your hearts?' In the
second story the criticism is outspoken, but not to Jesus
himself, only to his disciples. 'Why does he eat and drink
with tax collectors and sinners?' In the third and fourth
stories the criticisms are voiced directly to Jesus himself.
But they are still devious, for instead of criticizing Jesus
to the disciples they now criticize the disciples to Jesus.
'Why do . . . your disciples not fast?' And 'Why do they on
the sabbath day that which is not lawful?' Then at 3:1–6
the opposition develops from criticism directed towards
Jesus, to a deliberate plot against him. And when the
plot fails the religious leaders conspire with their
political opponents, the Herodians, 'how to destroy him.'
Hostility has reached its climax as far as Galilee is
concerned. But much worse is to come. At 3:22–35
hostility is widened to include the whole nation when
scribes come down from Jerusalem. At the same time
hostility is deepened to include even the mother and
brothers of Jesus.

In between the Specimen Day and these seven carefully
graded conflict stories, Mark has placed the Disobedient
Leper (1:40–45). 'Lord', cries the leper, 'if thou wilt thou
canst make me clean.' According to the most difficult,

and therefore most probably original text, this doubting of Jesus' willingness to heal, whilst acknowledging his power, arouses anger. Jesus tells him strictly to tell the cure to no one, *Hora mēdeni mēden eipēs*, but to show himself to the priest, and offer the due thanksgiving prescribed by Moses, 'for a testimony unto them'. This phrase, *eis martyrion autois*, is used again at 6:11, when the Twelve are bidden to testify to towns which refuse the gospel, and again at 13:9, where the disciples are to witness before rulers and kings.

But instead the cleansed leper makes the whole story public, and blazons it abroad so much that Jesus can no more openly enter the city. Instead he has to retreat to desert places, or to a ship, or to foreign parts or to anonymity. The leper has disobeyed both instructions of Jesus, concerning the priest and concerning the public. From this double disobedience Mark traces two currents of mounting trouble which combine to overwhelm the Galilean ministry: the opposition of the authorities, and the suffocating pressure of the crowds. Seven times Mark records the stifling encirclement of the multitude, at 1:45, 2:2, 3:9f, 4:1, 5:22-37, 6:31 and 7:24. Only one of these seven incidents is recorded by Matthew, and only two by Luke. In Mark the Galilean ministry is ground to a halt between the upper and nether millstones of official opposition and overwhelming popularity. And ironically both troubles stem from the irresponsible behaviour of a man healed by Jesus.

It is not hard to see the relevance of this when Mark's Gospel was written. Under Nero's persecution even the arrival of too many people at a meeting could arouse official suspicion. Christian testimony needed thought, discipline, and restraint.

At 3:7-12 Mark gives his fullest account of the overwhelming multitude, when all that had plagues rushed upon him, and a small ship had to be used as a refuge, 'lest they should persecute him'. The word for persecute, *thlibōsin*, is used again at 4:17 for persecution arising 'for the word's sake'. From this persecution Jesus escapes into a mountain. He regains the initiative by calling whom he would. To counter the pressure of a multitude demanding his presence all the time, he appoints twelve that they might be with him. To meet the ever widening demand for the good news, he ordains and empowers these twelve to preach. To prepare for the self-rejection of the old Israel, he creates the twelve partriarchs of his own new Israel. Their appointment takes place after the climax of opposition in Galilee, when Pharisees and Herodians combine to destroy him, and before the double climax when the opposition is enlarged to include the whole nation, the scribes from Jerusalem, and deepened to include even Jesus' own family. At 3:20, as soon as he leaves the mountain refuge, the overwhelming crowds return.

St. Matthew omits both Jesus' anger with the leper, and the leper's disobedience. So does St. Luke. But St. John returns to Mark's theme that it is possible for persecution to arise from Christian disobedience. As usual, John is more explicit than Mark. John deals with the rise of hostility, not in Galilee but in Jerusalem. Here the culprit is the cripple at the Pool of Bethesda, John 5:1–16. This man is cured anonymously, for Jesus 'conveyed himself away, a multitude being in that place'. He cannot tell the authorities who it was made him break the sabbath by carrying his bed. But afterwards Jesus revealed himself to the cripple in the temple, with the warning, 'Sin no more, lest a worse thing befall thee.' The cripple's response to Jesus' healing and self-disclosure is deliberately to give him away to his enemies. He is like the fool so vividly described in Ecclesiasticus 19, a compulsive conveyor of any information received. St. John, like St. Mark, understood that by giving himself to people, Jesus made himself vulnerable. 'And for this cause', says St. John, 'did the Jews persecute

Jesus, and sought to slay him, because he had done these
things on the sabbath day.' Here again, the indiscrimin-
ate use, even of good news, can raise a storm of envious
hostility.

The Cripple at Bethesda is a meaningful introduction
to St. John's Jerusalem conflict stories, just as the
Disobedient Leper is a meaningful introduction to St.
Mark's Galilean conflict stories. And the Appointment of
the Twelve has been placed in Mark's text where it can
be seen as Our Lord's countermeasure to the differing
problems raised by the leper's disobedience, the enmity of
the authorities and the mobbing of the multitude.

The Prologue Mark 1:1–20

Different commentaries on St. Mark locate the end of his
prologue at different places. But if it is granted that the
Typical Day, the Conflict, the Parable Teaching, and the
Miracle Stories form four clear sections, then we are
clearly left with Mark 1:1–20 for the initial section. The
theological value of this prologue becomes more evident
as the gospel unfolds. Its dramatic value is to reveal to
the readers at the outset the secret identity of Jesus,
which perplexes and judges the actors throughout the
drama. Thus we are given an aerial view of the mighty
conflicts about to be waged.

Perhaps Mark also intends his prologue to have a
practical value for the early Church. The emphasis
throughout these twenty verses is on the divine initiative. 'The beginning of the gospel of Jesus Christ the Son
of God ... was John baptizing in the wilderness.' God
prepares his way by sending the Forerunner, as he
promised in the Scriptures. Then God calls him to the
ministry. Then God tests his minister, driving him into
the wilderness. Then he gives the signal to begin. In this
case it is the imprisonment of the Forerunner. Then God

provides the fellow-workers, who are to be made fishers of men. All, from start to finish is by God's sovereign grace. God acts and his Son responds.

We can imagine what this meant, for instance to Alexander and Rufus, the two brothers mentioned by name at 15:21. Christ's commission is to take his gospel to their native Cyrenaica. But how on earth are they to begin? Mark's prologue tells them: 'You don't begin. God begins. You have to be ready to respond to his call, and submit to his training, and await his time. He will prepare the way before you, for it is his work you are doing'.

Mark 4:1–34

Mark's plan of placing Jesus' authoritative teaching before the miracles which vindicate it, is seen both in the synagogue at Capernaum and again in the order of the parable and miracle sections. It can also be seen in Matthew's Gospel. Matthew writes as a scribe instructed in the Kingdom of Heaven, a Christian rabbi. So he collates his Markan material with material from other sources into nine great teaching catenas. Seven of these are clearly expansions of teaching sections in Mark.[17] The other two contain material common to Matthew and Luke, so they could be classified as expansions of 'Q'.[18] Five of these teaching catenas end with the same formula: 'And it came to pass when Jesus had ended . . .' Accordingly Matthew begins his account of the Galilean ministry, not with a typical day in that ministry, but with the greatest of his nine teaching sections, Matthew 5–7, the Law of God interpreted by the Son of God. This is immediately followed by the greatest of Matthew's

17 Matthew 9:36–11:1; 12:24–45; 13:1–53; 19:16–20:16; 21:23–23:39; and 24:1–25:46.
18 Matthew 5–7 and 11:2–30.

miracle sections. Matthew 8:1–9:35 contains ten successive miracles and two collections of miracles, with only
two brief interludes. So Matthew follows the pattern
which Mark followed, both in his specimen day and in his
fourth and fifth sections: first the teaching with authority,
and then the signs which establish that authority.

Mark 4:1–34 is teaching about teaching. Its five
parables, the Sower, the Candlestick, the Just Measure,
the Seed growing Secretly, and the Mustard Seed, show
the many hindrances and the ultimate glorious triumph
of the gospel proclamation.

The three longer parables are about sowing and
growing. Their deeper meaning is disclosed by John
12:24, 'Except a corn of wheat fall into the ground and
die, it abideth alone; but if it die it bringeth forth much
fruit.' Jesus is the living Word of God, given like seed to a
death which issues in abundant life for many.[19] When
Mark wrote, Jesus' church under Nero was called upon to
suffer a similar fate, and by their witness unto death
make available for a still wider circle the salvation they
themselves had inherited from the Passion of their Lord.
The mystery of the Kingdom of God (4:11) is the paradox
of victory through self-sacrifice, of power by humiliation,
giving life by accepting death, fruitfulness by burial and
Resurrection.

At 4:11f we are told that the parables also have a
judgemental purpose. They serve to darken the damned
as well as to illumine the elect. But this is not a
judgement to be meekly accepted. Rather it is to be at all
costs avoided, like the warnings of the Old Testament
prophets which carried the implied proviso, 'Except ye
repent . . .' Mark makes this clear by making the
watchword of his parable section *Akouete* — 'Hearken

---

19 J.G. Williams: *Gospel against Parable, St. Mark's Language of
Mystery* (Sheffield 1986), 41–48.

and understand' — repeated like a warning storm-bell thirteen times in these thirty-four verses.

Mark 4:35–5:34

The miracles of 4:35–5:34 are a litany of triumph: 'From the worst violence of nature, from the worst powers of the devils, from disease no man could cure, and from death itself, the Good Lord does deliver us.' The phrase *para tēn thalassan*, beside the sea, at 5:21 links all four miracles to one region, giving them a unity of place as well as time.

The first five chapters of Mark could be summarized as follows:

1:1–20 How did the Galilean Ministry begin?
1:21–39 How was the Galilean Ministry conducted?
1:40–3:35 How did opposition arise?
4:1–34 How did Jesus enunciate his teaching in Galilee?
4:35–5:34 How did Jesus validate his teaching in Galilee?

CHAPTER SEVEN

THE STRUCTURE OF ST. MARK 6:1–8:30

In chapters 6–8 Mark's structure becomes mystifying. In this they are quite unlike the chapters which follow, where the Passion and its antecedents give a clear outline. They are also quite unlike chapters 1–5, where the sections on parables and on miracles, the prologue and the specimen day, are quite clear, and only the two additions to the conflict stories, the Disobedient Leper and the Appointment of the Twelve, needed explaining. In chapters 6–8 a great deal needs explaining. It is not at all clear why there are more conflict stories, more parables, and more miracles, outside the conflict, parable, and miracle sections. It is not clear why the healing miracles become more laborious and secretive, and why the lesser multitude feeding follows two chapters after the greater. It is not clear why Jesus and his disciples set out for Bethsaida, but land at Gennesaret, and why Jesus sets out from Tyre to the Sea of Galilee in a northerly direction.

In order to understand these chapters we need to look below the surface. We need to see the doctrinal as well as the historical significance of events. We need to observe the messages Mark signals by the way he edits and arranges and presents his stories. Once the doctrinal

significance of 6–8 is discerned, the anomalies cease to be
anomalous, and the structure of these chapters is just as
logical and just as meaningful as that of chapters 1–5 and
9–16.

In 1–5 the gospel of Jesus the Christ has been
proclaimed, first in words and then in deeds. But now
Mark goes on to explore deep mysteries. Why was this
proclamation rejected by Israel? Even the Twelve, chosen
to be the new Israel, can only (it appears) be brought to
full faith in the gospel by an agonizing struggle which
foretells and helps to explain the coming agony in
Jerusalem.

This central section of Mark opens with the dishonouring at Nazareth, 6:1–6. The scene is set in the synagogue,
just as it was in the initial description of the Galilean
ministry. The first reaction of the people at Nazareth is
exactly the same as at Capernaum. They were astonished
(*exeplēssonto*). Of the five different words used by Mark to
express astonishment, the same word is used at 6:2 as at
1:22. Amazement follows. But on this occasion the
positions are reversed. Instead of the *people* being
amazed at Jesus' power over a demon, it is *Jesus* himself
who is amazed at their unbelief.

Mark intends us to see in Nazareth's unbelief a
foreshadowing of the failure of Jesus' native country as a
whole to believe him. Mark shows this first, by placing
this incident at the very outset of his stories dealing with
the demise of the old Israel and birth of the new. And
secondly, by his use of the word *patris* for town at 6:1. He
does not use any of his usual words for a town, neither
polis, (city) nor *kōmē* (village) nor *kōmopolis*, but *patris*,
which can mean either 'native town' or 'native country'.

The Martyrdom of the Forerunner, which follows at
6:14–29, is equally suggestive of Israel's self-exclusion.
But this is dovetailed into the successful mission of the
Twelve, 6:7–13, 30. As the old Israel fails, the new Israel,
the faithful remnant, comes forward. The battle lines are

now drawn up. We know who will respond to the gospel and who will not. Therefore Jesus can now make his supreme self-disclosure in Galilee, the Feeding of the Five Thousand. This is the only miracle recorded in all four gospels, and it is crucial. To 'understand concerning the loaves' is to find full Christian faith. Mark presents the Feeding of the Five Thousand as the Messianic Banquet, the supreme revelation of Jesus' identity to those destined for salvation. So do St. Luke and St. John.

In St. Luke the Five Thousand leads directly to Peter's confession. St. John interposes the Walking on the Water, and Jesus' discourse with the multitude, the *ochlos*, on physical and spiritual bread. The reason for this is that the Five Thousand is treated by John, like Mark, as a farewell to the multitude as well as a sign to the Twelve. Mark simply states that Jesus dismissed the multitude and bade them farewell (*apoluei ton ochlon kai apotaxamenos autois*), before giving a further confirmation of his identity to the Twelve alone, namely the Walking on the Water. We do not fully understand why the crowd had to be dismissed at this point in Mark, until their character is exposed by their conduct at the trial before Pilate. There Mark uses the same Greek word, *ochlos*, for the crowd or mob who prefer Barabbas, and cry out for crucifixion. At this point we can see why the crowd were bidden farewell at 6:46.

As is so often the case, St. John makes clear what St. Mark leaves obscure. In St. John the *ochlos* follow Jesus to Capernaum, where we are shown just why they cannot be his. Jesus tells them plainly that they seek the physical bread which the miracle provided, instead of the spiritual bread which the miracle symbolized. When Jesus tries to explain to them that only the soul's food, which nourishes eternal life, is really worth labouring for, they walk no more with him. Jesus is left with the Twelve, and their spokesman makes his confession (John

6:22–69). John often elucidates in the text what Mark leaves to be expounded in the Church.

Mark has a very much longer interlude between the Five Thousand and Peter's confession, because he records problems which do not appear in Luke and John. Mark indicates that Jesus challenges the disciples' response to the Five Thousand immediately, as he walks on the waters. One indication of this challenge is that Jesus uses the divine title, '*Egō Eimi*', 'I AM', at 6:50. Another indication is the statement that Jesus 'wished to pass by them' on the water, *ēthelen parelthein autous. Parelthein* is the verb used in the Septuagint for the Lord 'passing by' in his appearance to Moses (Exodus 33:22), and again in his appearance to Elijah (1 Kings 19:11).

By contrast, Job fails to perceive this theophany: 'He alone spreadeth out the heavens, and treadeth upon the waves of the sea . . . Lo, he goeth by me and I see him not; he passeth on also (*parelthē*, LXX), but I perceive him not' (Job 9:8–11).

In Matthew's account the Twelve do not fail to make the response which Jesus clearly seeks: 'Then all that were in the ship came and worshipped him, saying, "Of a truth thou art the Son of God"'.

But in Mark's account their faith fails. The disciples are dumbfounded, and the reason is plainly stated: 'They understood not concerning the loaves, for their hearts were hardened.' The same word *pōrōsis*, meaning 'hardening', is used at Romans 11:7 for the hardening or blinding of Israel 'until the fulness of the Gentiles be come in'. At Mark 3:5 Jesus is angry and grieved at the *pōrōsis*, 'hardness of heart', of the critics in the synagogue. Now even the Twelve display *pōrōsis*.

Mark wishes his readers to understand the seriousness of the situation. He has recounted the dishonouring at Nazareth, and linked the slaughter of the Baptist with the mission of the Twelve, he has shown how the dismissal of the multitude was followed by a second theophany to the Twelve alone. It is clear that Israel has been blinded to the presence of God's Only Beloved Son, and that everything now depends on the Twelve. Until the 'cardiac *pōrōsis*' of the Twelve is cured all is lost.

Opening the eyes of the Twelve

Mark's next two chapters therefore portray the agonizing struggle of Jesus to cure his disciples' hardening or blinding. Passages in these chapters so closely resemble earlier ones that they have been stigmatized as 'doublets'. But a closer examination shows that Mark is deliberately describing a second laying on of hands for blinded eyes. At 6:45 the disciples were ordered to sail to *Bethsaida*. But at 6:53 they land at *Gennesaret*. Their tragic failure on the journey has altered their destination! Bethsaida is to be the city where a blind man's eyes are opened by a second laying on of hands (8:22–26). Immediately after this miracle the disciples' eyes are at last opened to the truth (8:27–30).

We are not told precisely why Bethsaida is to be the place where blindness is cured. We do know that it was outside the jurisdiction of Herod Antipas, the murderer of the Baptist, and that it was on the road to Caesarea Philippi. Matthew and Luke tell us that it was the scene of mighty miracles, and John that it was the native city of Andrew, Peter and Philip.

But because the disciples 'considered not the miracle of the loaves, for their heart was hardened' at 6:52, they could not yet go forward to the city of enlightenment. Instead, Jesus had to take them back to the plain of Gennesaret in Herod's Galilee, to cure their hardness of heart by repetition, given with infinitely patient love, of all the signs of Christhood. They go back to the vast crowds and insupportable work-load (6:53–56). Back to the bitter struggle with unreal religion (7:1–13). Back to

the parable teaching, (7:14–23). Back to the miracles of
exorcism and healing, even though these now have to be
performed outside Israel, and with increasing labour and
danger (7:24–37). Finally the Messianic Feast itself is re-
enacted, though this time with fewer people fed, with
greater initial resources, and with less superabundance
at the end (8:1–9). Then, after the Four Thousand, Jesus
categorically refuses to give a sign from heaven 'unto this
generation'. The language here reflects the Septuagint
account of the Exodus generation who tempted God
by their unbelief. Jesus' deep sigh in spirit, and his
emphatic, 'Verily I say . . .' underline that we have
reached the end of the road. Every sign that can possibly
be given has now been vouchsafed (8:10–13).

Accordingly, immediately after the refusal of a sign,
Jesus makes an impassioned plea to his disciples in the
ship, to respond to the signs already given (8:14–21). He
begins by bidding them beware of the leaven of the
Pharisees, who ascribed his miracles to collusion with
the devil, and of Herod, who explained him as a revival of
John the Baptist. But the disciples are still obtuse. Jesus
cries in desperation: 'Perceive ye not yet, neither understand? Have ye your heart yet hardened? Having eyes,
see ye not? And having ears, hear ye not?' These
questions echo the words of Jesus at 4:12, when he said of
those outside, *tois exō*, '. . . that seeing they may see, and
not perceive, and hearing they may hear and not
understand'. But now the wilful blindness and deafness
which damned those outside, threaten even the Twelve.
Hardening of the heart will slay the last hope of
humanity unless they can be made to see the significance
of the multitude feedings. Jesus continues: 'Do ye not
remember? When I brake the five loaves among the five
thousand, how many clothes baskets of fragments took ye
up? . . . And the seven among the four thousand, how
many shopping baskets of fragments took ye up? . . . How
is it that ye do not yet understand?' Jesus deliberately

calls the baskets of fragments after the five thousand *kophinoi*, (6:43), and the baskets after the four thousand *spyrides*, (8:8), the point being that the *kophinoi* held more. (To 'kophinate' someone was to place a big basket right over him, to signify that he could not meet his debts, and was barred from trading.) The substance of Jesus' argument here is that the feeding of the four thousand was less miraculous in every respect. The number fed this second time was smaller, and even though the resources available for them at the beginning were greater, the remainder at the end was very much less. The Feeding of the Four Thousand was still stupendous compared with Old Testament times, when Elisha fed a hundred men with twenty loaves, and had some left, at 2 Kings 4:42–44. Even so, the sands are running out. The daylight is fading. Hence the urgency of Jesus' plea for sight before the day ends. Unless the Twelve recognize their divine visitor now, and find full faith in him, mankind is lost.

The length and intensity of Jesus' pleading reveal the terrible strain upon him. 'Have ye your heart yet hardened?' foreshadows in Galilee the cry of 'lama sabachthani' in Judaea. But this last desperate appeal is not in vain, for we are told in the very next verse: 'And he cometh to Bethsaida.'

Professor R.H. Lightfoot has pointed out that the healing of the blind man of Bethsaida is in six points parallel to the confession which follows. The blind man is taken aside privately for his anointing and laying on of hands. A first question is put. A dim answer is given. A second laying on of hands and a second question follow. The blind man sees clearly. He is ordered to secrecy.[20]

The gift of physical sight at Bethsaida presages the gift of physical sight at Caesarea Philippi. And both are

20 R.H. Lightfoot: *History and Interpretation of the Gospels* (London 1935) 90f.

structured in the same way as Mark's Gospel itself from
6:30. Here the Apostles gather themselves together unto
Jesus, and Jesus stretches out his hands, as it were, to
give them spiritual sight by the signs of the Five
Thousand and the Walking on the Waters. But terror
holds the Twelve back from the truth. A second laying on
of hands is needed, and this is shown by Mark to be
arduous and increasingly costly. The second multitude
feeding is less in every respect than the first. And the last
two healing miracles before Peter's confession, the Deaf–
mute of Decapolis and the Blind Man of Bethsaida, are
more laborious and dangerous. Hitherto a word or a
touch has sufficed to cure. But now considerable ritual
and anointing with the healer's saliva are needed. And
both miracles have to be concealed by withdrawal into
privacy before the cure and strict commands to secrecy
afterwards. Mark is showing us how hardly we are saved.

The Secrecy Motif

To understand why these two miracles are concealed, we
need to examine briefly the secrecy motif throughout
Mark's Gospel. William Wrede and his followers interpreted the commands to secrecy as an attempt to reconcile post-resurrection Christology with pre-resurrection
history, and explain why Jesus was not recognized as Son
of God in his life-time. But in doing so they overlooked
two important facts in Mark's text. The first fact is that
in the last six of Mark's sixteen chapters the 'Messianic
secret' is a secret no longer. It is right out in the open.
The second fact is that the demons who know who Jesus
is, and the humans who witness Jesus' miracles, are
silenced in very different ways, and for different reasons,
making two distinct and unrelated secrecy 'problems'.[21]

---

21 W. Wrede: *Das Messiasgeheimnis in den Evangelein* (1913[2]; ET
The Messianic Secret, Cambridge 1971).

The concealment of some of the healing miracles begins with the disobedient leper at 1:40–45, who is told to keep his cure a secret from all but the priest. When the leper fails to obey, publicity spells danger. And yet, of the eleven other healing miracles recorded in full in Mark's Gospel, only three are preceded by seclusion and followed by orders not to tell others. One is the supreme miracle, the raising of the dead. The others are the last two before Caesarea Philippi. By contrast, the paralysed man at 2:3–12 was ordered to demonstrate his cure 'before them all'; the man with a withered hand at 3:3 to 'arise in the midst'. And the demoniac in Decapolis, where perhaps the danger from publicity was less than in Galilee, was actually told to tell others (5:19). The careful concealing of the last two cures before Peter's confession therefore illustrates the great danger involved, just as the elaborate ritual illustrates the great difficulty involved, in curing the disciples' hardness of heart. St Mark is underlining the intensity of Jesus' struggle to bring the new Israel to faith.

In sharp contrast to the partial and occasional concealment of Jesus' miraculous cures, the demons who try to reveal Jesus' identity are invariably and totally silenced. The imperfect tenses *ēthien* at 1:34 and *epetima* at 3:12 indicate settled practice: 'He used to forbid the devils to speak because they knew him.' The unclean spirit in the synagogue at Capernaum knew him to be 'the Holy One of God' who had come to destroy the devils. The demons in the summarizing section at 3:11 knew him as 'the Son of God'. The Gerasene demoniac called him 'the Son of God Most High'. The substance of the demons' revelations was never at fault. It was their timing. Their disclosure was premature until the time came when the cross revealed its true meaning. Jesus refuses to be given his name until the Passion has revealed his nature. Then, and only then, the way into the Holy of Holies is opened to all. To confess Christ crucified by men but

raised by God involved a reversal of values, a death to the
world, a revolutionary new thinking and living. But to
identify Jesus before his rejection involved no such
change, no self-emptying and God-filling. The demons
would have put Jesus at the right hand of power before
his Passion had revealed the utmost of his self-giving
love. It was after Jesus had been damned by the religious
leaders, exiled by his prince, and disowned even by his
family, that he invited his disciples to confess that he was
nevertheless the Christ. And then he immediately began
to teach them that this title involved the ultimate
rejection of the cross. Only so could men come to distrust
all things human, and totally trust in God who raises his
Son from the dead. The devils' premature disclosure
would have upset this plan of salvation.

Therefore when the Twelve came to share the devils'
secret, they too were silenced (8:30) but only until Jesus
began his ascent to Calvary, and openly shared his secret
with friends and foes. Six days later, when the truth of
Peter's confession was confirmed by heaven at the
Transfiguration, the three witnesses were silenced, but
only until the Resurrection, which the Transfiguration
foretold (9:9). By that time Jesus will have openly
asserted his messianic authority in the temple, and
suffered in consequence. By his death Jesus will reveal
the uttermost of God's love and of man's need, and then
his authority as ruler and judge of the world can be
revealed also. Jesus can be personally worshipped without idolatry. The full gospel can be proclaimed.

The silencing of the demons in Galilee, and of the
disciples when they learn the demons' secret, serves
Mark's declared purpose of recording the good news of
Jesus the Christ the Son of God. So does the concealment
of three of the healing miracles. If St. Mark's purpose had
been apologetic, to explain why Jesus was not recognized
as the Christ in his life-time, St. Mark would not have
made such a difference between the silencing of the

demons and the concealing of some miracles. And he would not have recorded the disappearance of messianic secrecy when Jesus came to Jerusalem. Mark's purpose is not apologetic but evangelical, to explain the necessity for the cross, and how it mediates eternal life to believers. Until Mark's theological purpose is understood, his narrative does indeed read like a collection of beads without a string. The string is the gospel.

Rejection by Israel: Blessing for the Gentiles

Several critics have suggested that there is a subsidiary theme at Mark 7:1–8:9, namely the opening of the Kingdom of God to the Gentiles. Jesus' liberalizing and rationalizing of the food laws at 7:1–23 is followed by an exorcism in Syrophoenicia and a healing in Decapolis. These in turn are followed by a second feeding of the multitude, divers of whom came from far. St. Paul in Romans 11 explains how Israel's temporary rejection of the gospel has led, in the providence of God, to the inclusion of the Gentiles. Here we have a forecast of this when Jesus ministers to other nations when he has been rejected by his own. Mark has been accused of muddled geography at 7:31: 'And coming again from the territory of Tyre, he came through Sidon to the Sea of Galilee through the midst of the territory of Decapolis'. But if Jesus is being portrayed as an exile, giving Herod's Galilee as wide a berth as possible, the geography at 7:31 is exactly right. Sidon was north of Tyre. The western shores of Galilee were in Herod's tetrarchy, the northeastern in Philip's and the southeastern in Decapolis. By placing the rejection at Nazareth, and the murder of the Baptist by Herod together at the beginning of this section, Mark implies that Jesus has gone into exile when he has said farewell to the crowds and travelled into heathen territory. He does not return into Galilee

except in secret. But by Jesus' avoidance of Galilee the
Gentiles are blessed. He is like crumbs of soul food falling
by mistake from the children's table.

Mark brings in other themes, as he did by his three
parentheses in the conflict stories. But his main theme
throughout chapters 6–8 is to present a Galilean pre-
passion, as it were. Chapter 6 shows Jesus spurned,
rejected, and cast out of the vineyard. At the same time
the successful mission of the Twelve shows that they are
to be the faithful remnant. When even the Twelve fail to
respond to the Feeding of the Five Thousand and the
Walking on the Waters, because their hearts were
hardened, the situation for the whole world is desperate.
Chapters 7 and 8 portray an agonizing struggle to bring
the Twelve to full faith. The battle is won at last, not in
faithless Galilee, but at Caesarea Philippi.

CHAPTER EIGHT

THE STRUCTURE OF ST. MARK
8:31–10:45

After their discovery that Jesus is the Christ, the Twelve
are given no time to simply bask in their enlightenment.
They cannot just revel in the cure of their *pōrōsis*, for
Jesus immediately tells them the consequences of his
Christhood, that he must suffer many things and be
rejected ... Indeed, unless and until he suffers many
things and is rejected and killed, he cannot function as
the opener of the Holy of Holies, the link between God
and man. The temple made without hands where all the
world can worship is to be built by his Passion. Until he
overcomes the sharpness of death and opens the kingdom
of God to all believers, the disciples must keep his
identity a secret (8:30).

A Threefold Pattern

Therefore from Caesarea Philippi their road must go to
Jerusalem. The journey to Jerusalem provides the framework for this part of the gospel (8:27–10:52), and the
framework helps us to interpret the exciting and un-
expected incidents along the road. At 8:27 Jesus asks his
disciples, 'Whom say ye that I am?' in the way, *en tē hodō*.
And this same phrase, *en tē hodō*, recurs at each stage of

63

the journey. After a second prediction of the Passion
Jesus asks the Twelve, 'What was it ye disputed among
yourselves in the way?' A third prediction takes place 'in
the way going up to Jerusalem'. Finally, at the end of the
journey we meet blind Bartimaeus sitting *beside* the
way, *para tē hodon.* Beside the way is where the
unfruitful seed fell in the parable of the Sower at 4:4 and
4:15. But when sight has been miraculously given by
Jesus, Bartimaeus follows him *in* the way, *en tē hodō.*
The same word 'Way' is used in Acts to signify the
Christian movement.

At three clear points on the journey, at Caesarea
Philippi, in Galilee, and at the ascent to Jerusalem from
beyond Jordan, Jesus predicts his Passion and Resurrection. Each prediction is more detailed than the one
before. The second prediction contains the dreaded word
paradidōmi, 'betray' or 'deliver up'. The third contains
it twice. Paradidōmi is used in the Septuagint for the
betrayal or handing over of King Zedekiah to his enmies
the Babylonians by his own subjects, at Jeremiah 38:19f.
When Mark wrote, the prophecy of 13:12, that the
disciples would be betrayed or delivered up to their
persecuters by their own brothers or fathers or children,
was being tragically fulfilled under Nero.

Each of the three predictions is followed by some moral
failure on the part of the disciples, showing their
blindness to the truth that the road of the cross is the
road of light: 'via crucis, via lucis'. In turn these failures
provide Jesus with an opportunity to give more teaching
about cross-bearing in daily life, so that the spiritual
journey to self-surrender proceeds in parallel with the
geographical journey to the literal Mount Zion.

Canon John Fenton has pointed out that the contrast
in Mark 9:49 is between the demands of the Law and the
demands of the Kingdom. The Law requires that every
sacrifice be salted with salt. The Lord requires that every
person be salted with fire. Through the fire that destroys

lies the highway to the life that lasts. This is a constant theme in Mark's Gospel, and especially in this central teaching section, 8:31–10:45.

The care with which Mark adheres to his structure in this section can be seen by comparison with Matthew and Luke. Matthew inserts another story about St. Peter, the coin in the fish's mouth (Matthew 17:24–27), which does not involve disciple-failure, and therefore interrupts the pattern. Luke obscures the pattern by adding almost nine of his twenty-four chapters between the second and third predictions. St. Mark carefully fills the interlude between the first and second predictions with three stories, and the interlude between the second and third predictions with three stories.

After the first prediction and its teaching Mark gives the Transfiguration on the mount, the discourse on Elijah on the way down, and the healing of the epileptic boy in the valley, which is a foil to the vision in the heights. Together these three stories set the seal of heaven on Peter's confession and all that has been achieved in Galilee, whilst pointing forward to its necessary fulfilment in Jerusalem. The Transfiguration takes place 'after six days' from Peter's confession. The Resurrection takes place after exactly the same interval from the people's confession on Palm Sunday.

After the second prediction and its teaching, three delegations meet Jesus as he enters Judaea, (1) Pharisees, (2) parents, and (3) the rich man. If these three stories are here for a purpose, like all the other incidents on the journey, that purpose is not altogether clear.

Perhaps they forecast what is about to happen in Judaea. (1) The religious leaders will argue and oppose. (2) The little ones will seek Jesus' blessing, and will be blessed despite human hindrance. (3) The rich and powerful will come running, but will not pay the price. We can see from these three stories what will happen in the southern province, and why.

Perhaps also these stories give three glimpses into the Kingdom of God which Jesus has come to offer. (1) The sexes will live together in the fidelity and felicity which was theirs before the fall, and in equality. (2) Even the smallest humans will be rightly valued. And (3) riches will have no value at all until transmuted into spiritual wealth by right use.

When human nature fails

The three disciples whose failings are recorded after the three predictions of the Passion are Peter, James and John. These are the three placed first in the list of the Twelve; the three given surnames, as Abram and Jacob were surnamed in the Old Testament; the three chosen to witness the raising of the dead and the Transfiguration. The failure of the three men closest to him to march with Jesus God's road to passion and victory, portrays as nothing else could the loneliness of Jesus, and his anguish at our unfaith. This theme is continued at 14:33–42, where the same three fail to support him in his crucial spiritual combat in Gethsemane. But at 13:3, when Jesus next has truth to impart in private to chosen disciples, those chosen are different by the addition of Andrew. To have recorded just the same three where no failure was involved would have upset a careful editorial pattern.

Some critics have argued that Mark records the failures of Peter, James and John because they were pillars of the Church in Jerusalem, which opposed the admission of uncircumcised Gentiles. Also that the failure of Jesus' mother and brothers is recorded at 3: 21–35 because they too were Judaisers, opposed to the liberal policy of Mark and Paul. With all the sects and parties of Jewry already in opposition, such an interpretation would give Mark so many enemies as to reduce his book from a gospel with power to save to a cheap and embittered polemic. But the contexts in which Mark has placed these failures makes such an interpretation impossible. If Mark had meant to put down the first three disciples, he would never have begun by lauding them to the heights as first in the list of apostles, surnamed, and chosen for the most sublime tasks.

As Mark writes for church members, Peter, the disciple most severely faulted in Mark's Gospel, would be known to his readers as the triumphant apostle of Acts. After Pentecost Peter reversed his denials before the very same tribunal. He escaped from Herod's dungeon. He performed mighty miracles, even raising the dead. He played a major part in taking the gospel out to the Gentiles. Peter had just crowned a glorious ministry in Rome with an heroic martyrdom. All the churches believed that he was crucified upside down at his own request, lest his should be confused with the only perfect sacrifice. St. Mark is contrasting the former weaknesses of the disciples with the strength Jesus gave them by his Passion and Resurrection and the gift of his Holy Spirit. By portraying the needs of those who were acknowledged to be the very best of men, Mark reveals the greater needs of lesser men. He is not trying to smear his opponents, but to save his readers. That is why he allows the disciples to be the black backdrop against which the dazzling perfection of Jesus is seen to the best advantage. The implication is plain. If even the three best of the twelve apostles failed so signally, how much more does our human nature need the transformation which can only be found at Calvary?

St. Mark treats Jesus' kin in the same way as Jesus' disciples. In 1 Corinthians 9:5 the brothers of Jesus are listed with the apostles who travelled with their wives in the service of the gospel, and were entitled to the support of the churches. The character and achievements of Jesus' brothers after Pentecost were not unknown to Mark's readers. So when Mark records their attempt to

apprehend Jesus as a madman, he dovetails their failure
with that of the top-ranking scribes, the scribes from
Jerusalem. Always Mark shows the inadequacy of the
best. It is the scribes most famed for wisdom who make
the gravest doctrinal error: 'He casteth out devils by
Beelzebub.' And it is those closest to Jesus, physically
and emotionally, who rate his work most abysmally: 'He
is beside himself.' Mark's irony has an evangelical
purpose, to show how very far short the very best fall
below God's requirement, as shown by God's Son, and
what a change is wrought when they accept the verdict of
Calvary and the power of the Holy Spirit.

The same theme, the shortfall of man's best, appears
again in the two trials of Jesus. Mark has been accused of
trying to shift the blame for the crucifixion from the
Romans to the Jews. But in fact he presents the failure of
Roman justice as just as total and just as terrible as the
failure of Jewish religion. Pilate knows that the Council
have 'delivered up' Jesus for envy, and that he has done
no evil. And yet to content the mob he 'delivers up' the
innocent to scourging and crucifixion. Virgil in the
Aeneid describes justice as the special gift of the Romans,
with which they were endowed by heaven for their
appointed task of ruling the nations.[22] Mark shows how
even Roman justice, and even Jewish religion, both
reputed to be the world's very best, both fail abysmally
when judged by the Christ.

Alike in his account of the two trials, and in his dovetail
of the error of Jesus' family with that of the scribes from
Jerusalem, and in his many stories of the disciples'
shortcomings, St. Mark records failure, not to fault
theological opponents, but to present a gospel. He con-
demns even the best that this fallen world can achieve
without the grace of God mediated by the life and Passion

22 Virgil: *Aeneid Book 6* 757–853, especially 850–853.

and Resurrection of Jesus. He pleads a total distrust in our own resources, and a total trust in God's willingness to forgive and ability to save. For Mark, the *evangelion*, the good news or gospel, is not complete until all man's need is revealed, as well as all God's love, by the cross; and the glory of God's purpose for man by the Resurrection. Mark portrays the extent of this need by showing the gap between God's design and the utmost the best people on earth can achieve without him. That is why he brings to the judgement of the Christ the chiefest of the apostles, the closest of Jesus' kin, the religion of the Jews and the justice of the Romans.

In Mark's theology the cross of Christ is not only the measure of God's love for us. It is also the measure of our need for God. So in his passion narrative Mark highlights the part played in the blackest deed in all human history by Jewish religion and by Roman law; by Iscariot and Peter, two of the twelve chosen disciples, and by the multitude.

CHAPTER NINE

THE STRUCTURE OF ST. MARK
10:46–13:37

At 10:32–45 the most detailed prediction of the Passion is followed by the clearest explanation of the Passion. Then comes a curious double emphasis that Jesus has entered Jericho and left it: 'And they came to Jericho. And as he went out of Jericho with his disciples and a great multitude . . .'.

Jericho is a great turning point on the journey, because as soon as Jesus leaves Jericho he comes out into the open. Hitherto his identity as the Christ, the Son of God, has been a closely guarded secret. Always the demons who know the secret have been silenced. And so have the Twelve as soon as they too learn the secret. But now the messianic secret is openly proclaimed, and the messianic authority accorded to Jesus is openly exercized in the temple. From Jericho Jesus begins his royal ascent to his Calvary throne and crown of thorns. First Bartimaeus, the man whose eyes are opened by the gift of God, hails him as Son of David, and responds to Jesus' call, casting aside his robe. Then, as they near Jerusalem, the whole multitude take up the cry. They too sacrifice their robes, to give him messianic acclaim. Jesus shows them the kind of Messiah he is destined to be by mounting an ass's colt. He is destined to have dominion to the ends of the earth, and establish peace, as foretold at Zechariah 9:9f.

But only Jesus knows the means whereby he will bring heaven's peace to earth's end, namely by total self-sacrifice. Three times he has told the Twelve this terrible secret, but they have been unable to grasp it. In the midst of the mighty multitude Jesus is utterly alone.

Messianic Authority

Throughout this section events move logically and swiftly and inevitably to the strange climax which Jesus alone foresees. Jesus' messianic authority as Son of David:

1. Is seen by 'blind' Bartimaeus (10:46–52).
2. Is acclaimed at the triumphal entry (11:1–11).
3. Is exercised in the temple (11:13–26).
4. Is challenged by the chief priests and scribes and elders (11:27f).
5. Is fully vindicated through the Day of Questions (11:29–12:44).

Jesus' counter-question about the Baptism of John shows how the chief priests and scribes have lost their right to question Jesus' authority. John's prophetic call to Israel demanded an answer. When the authorities failed to give any answer, neither Yes nor No, they forfeited their right to decide who spoke for God, and who did not. They resigned from their office. Therefore Jesus is no longer answerable to them (11:29–33).

Next the parable of the Wicked Husbandmen presents Our Lord's counter-challenge. Jesus assumes the supreme title given him by God himself, at his Baptism and at his Transfiguration, 'My unique beloved Son' (*ho huios mou ho agapētos*). His coming is Israel's supreme test. To reject him is national disaster (12:1–9).

Then the parable of the Head Corner-stone demon-

strates from scripture that God will reverse the rejection
of his Son (12:10f).

Next Jesus' authority is assailed, first from the political
angle, by the question of tribute to Caesar; and then from
the theological angle by the question about the Resurrection. His gospel is found to be both politically and
theologically unassailable (12:13–27).

Thereafter Jesus is supreme in the temple, and holds
the keys. He judges who is not far from the Kingdom of
God, and whose heart is pure (12:28–34; 12:41–44). He
demolishes both the teaching and the conduct of the
scribes (12:35–40).

Totally defeated in the battle of words, his enemies can
only take up arms.

The 'Little Apocalypse'

But in between these Jerusalem conflict stories and their
logical outcome, the Passion story, St. Mark has placed
a strange interlude, a forward look into a terrifying
future, the so-called Little Apocalypse (13:1–37). Dr. G.R.
Beasley-Murray has pointed out that the normal place
for eschatological instruction in early Christian cate-
chesis is at the end, as in the Sermon on the Mount, and
in Paul's epistles, and at Mark 8:27–9:1. A more natural
place for a look into the future would be the forty days
when the risen Christ showed himself alive, and spake of
the things pertaining to the Kingdom of God.[23]

To understand why Mark's Little Apocalypse comes
here, and breaks into the orderly development of Mark's
narrative, it is necessary to look briefly at its contents.
There are four introductory verses, placing this prophecy

23 G.H. Beasley-Murray: 'Second Thoughts on the Composition of
Mark Thirteen', *Journal of New Testament Studies* (July 1983)
414–420.

on the Mount of Olives, where the Lord will appear as saviour and judge of Jerusalem in the prophecy of Zechariah 14:1–20. Thereafter seven verses are devoted to the coming destruction of Jerusalem, and four to the Parousia, but no fewer than twenty-two verses to the right response of Christians to such crises. The theme of the chapter is set by a fivefold *blepete* ('Open your eyes'), followed by a threefold *Grēgoreite*, ('Keep alert'). The temple buildings have opened the eyes of the disciples wide in wonder. But these buildings are to be utterly destroyed, in tumultuous times in which they must open their eyes to the deceits of counterfeit Christs (13:5–8). Indeed they must open their eyes to their own spiritual resources, for they will face bitterest persecution, betrayal by their own nearest and dearest, and the hatred of all men (13:9–13). Even after the tribulations of the Jewish War have been providentially shortened, they must still keep their eyes open for pseudo-christs and pseudo-prophets (13:14–23). They must open their eyes for the signs, foretold by the prophets, of the coming Parousia, as a fig tree owner watches for the growth of leaf and bud as signs of the harvest to come (13:24–31). More than this, they must be watchful and alert for the sudden denouement for which no warning signs are possible, as servants whose lord may return at any time of the day or night, and keep alert at all times. The word for keep alert, *grēgoreite*, is used three times in the next chapter for keeping alert in prayer in Gethsemane (13:32–37).

All this reverses the policy of those apocalyptic writers, from Daniel onwards, who sought to comfort the persecuted with promises of good times and favourable judgements just around the corner. On the contrary, Jesus here warns against easy solutions, and prophesies worse trials ahead, to be met with no self-delusion and no recrimination, but with dauntless faith, and the alertness of him who refused drugged wine at Golgotha. Mark

13 might be styled an anti-apocalypse. Because it prepares the disciples for their own passion, it has no place thematically in the Easter triumph. Instead it is intruded between the Jerusalem conflict complex and the Passion of Jesus — for men called to follow their Lord through the Church's darkest hour.

Mark writes for a church accused of complicity in the burning of Rome, the penalty for which was to be made into human torches to illuminate the nocturnal games in the Imperial Gardens or the Vatican Circus. No wonder Mark 13 alerts disciples against false Christs and false prophets, with their facile hopes and recriminatory promises. Mark's own answer to the Church's testing under Nero is an increase of faith, to match the challenge of the forces of evil. In no fewer than eight of his miracle stories he records that faith was the factor which brought salvation. Mark alone records that lack of faith prevented the miracles at Nazareth. He alone gives the poignant words of the distraught father of the epileptic boy at 9:24: 'Lord, I believe. Help thou mine unbelief.' Whereas St. John, writing in more spacious times, records Jesus' passionate pleading for unity, (John 17:11–26), St. Mark, writing from the furnace of adversity, records his passionate pleading for faith (8:14–21).

St. Mark spares no pains to impress upon his readers that the horrors they are called upon to face under Nero were endured in full measure by their Lord, and that the Kingdom of God could come in no other way. He uses the bitter blackness of his times to make plain for all time the full horror of sin and the full splendour of God's love. When the infant Christian Church was accused of burning Rome, circa AD 67, a hurricane of hatred and ferocity was unleashed without parallel in history — except perhaps when the innocent Jews were accused of causing the Black Death in 1348. Mark 13 gives us the response of Christ's apostles through their intepreter.

Miraculously, their reaction is utterly free from vindictiveness against Rome, as it is utterly free from false hopes of an immediate Day of Judgement. Instead, Christians are bidden to face their darkest hour as Jesus faced his cross, with serene faith that their sufferings were God's way of gaining heaven and revealing his love to the world.

CHAPTER TEN

THE STRUCTURE OF ST. MARK
14:1–16:8

Much of Mark's skill in structuring the Passion story has already been shown in the chapters on dovetailing, irony and titles. He begins the narrative with two dovetails which sharply contrast human wickedness and weakness with the divine love which heals them. First, the anointing at Bethany is dovetailed between the murderous plotting of the Council, and their bribery of Judas. Second, the gift of the eucharist is dovetailed between Jesus' two prophecies of the moral breakdown of his disciples, Judas' betrayal and Peter's denial. The powers of good and evil are about to engage in their ultimate conflict.

Each of the two trials has its false accusation. At the Jewish trial Jesus is accused of threatening to destroy the temple, and rebuild it in three days. At the Roman trial he is accused of claiming to be king of the Jews. Both accusations are deeply ironic; the accusers speak more truly than they can possibly know. After each trial the irony is heightened when each false accusation is turned into bitter mockery.

At the crucifixion Mark makes another curious repetition. 15:24 records that Jesus was crucified and his garments divided amongst the soldiers. Then the next verse repeats: 'And it was the third hour (9 a.m.) and they crucified him'. John corrects Mark at this point, saying that Jesus was condemned at the sixth hour (12 noon). This was theologically important to John because it was the hour when the sacrifice of the Passover lambs began. So why was the third hour so emphasized by Mark? It seems to be part of his pattern. In Holy Week events are recorded each day, but in the Passion itself at the three–hourly Roman watches of the day:

> In the evening Jesus comes to the Last Supper.
> In the night he comes to Gethsemane, to arrest and desertion and trial.
> At cock-crow he is denied.
> In the early morning he is 'handed over' to Pilate.
> At the third hour he is crucified.
> At the sixth hour there is darkness.
> At the ninth hour he wins the victory.
> In the evening he is buried.

Four of these same Roman watches were enumerated at 13:35 by Jesus himself, when he warned his disciples that the lord of the household might return 'at even, or at midnight, or at cock-crow, or in the early morning.'

This measured ordering of events all through the Passion story is combined with frequent indications of scriptural prophecy come true, to convey a strong impression that God is overruling the whole drama, triumphant through tragedy.

Compare the three predictions of the Passion, and the three slumberings in Gethsemane, leading to three denials. The pattern of events begins to be completed on the third day, when three women discover the empty tomb. In Mark the measured ordering of the time sequence is a symbol of heavenly control over earthly events.

Mark's structure at 16:1–8 is reminiscent of the

conclusion to the first half of the book. Just as Peter's confession was confirmed from heaven by the Transfiguration, so the centurion's confession is confirmed by the Resurrection. Just as Peter totally misunderstood the Transfiguration, so the women at the tomb fail to comprehend the Resurrection. Divine truth is too dazzling for human eyes.

But did Mark really intend to finish his Gospel at 16:8, with the women still perplexed and fearful and disobedient? Or did some misfortune, such as the arrest of St. Peter perhaps, or the arrest of Mark himself, or the sudden need to hide the scroll and escape, prevent the evangelist from adding the resurrection appearances so clearly foretold at 14:28 and again at 16:7? All three predictions of the Passion end in predictions of the Resurrection also. And if Peter's confession was confirmed by an appearance of Christ in glory, how much more does the centurion's confession need confirming by actual Resurrection appearances, if the pattern is to be completed? But ever since R.H. Lightfoot suggested that 16:8 might have been St. Mark's intended ending, the question has been fiercely debated, and remains one of the unsolved mysteries of the second gospel.[24] We can only be eternally grateful that both St. Matthew and St. Luke may be numbered among those who felt that the gospel could not end abruptly at 16:8. Both felt that Resurrection appearances must be added to Mark's account, together with birth stories and so many priceless treasures of dominical teaching.

St. Mark portrays the triumph of the truth over the darkest tragedy in the Church's history. It is the measure of his genius to convey that triumph through the

---

24 R.H. Lightfoot: *The Gospel Message of St. Mark* (Oxford 1950) Ch.7.

ministry and Passion of Jesus, even though prevented
from recording the Resurrection.

Even the most tragic and sombre utterance in the
whole of Mark's Gospel, the cry of dereliction from the
cross at 15:34, is the beginning of a psalm which ends in
high triumph. See especially Psalm 22:27: 'All the ends of
the world shall remember and turn unto the Lord, and all
the kindreds of the nations shall worship before Thee'.
The triumphant outcome of the bitter suffering is only
clear after interpretation by Christian expositors with
the Old Testament at their finger tips. Without the
expositor all is dark. This is Mark's style throughout. His
Gospel is full of dark mysteries of failure and of injustice,
and instead of giving a full solution at the outset, Mark
simply indicates where the solution is to be found. He
leaves room for the Christian expositor. Hence his purpose is better served by the quotation of four Aramaic
words from the opening verse of Psalm 22, than it would
be by the quotation of the whole psalm. Compare Jesus'
answer to the High Priest's question at his trial, Mark
14:62. Two very brief scriptural quotations, just five
words from Psalm 110, followed by six from Daniel 7,
indicate how an expositor skilled in the Scriptures could
transform the darkness of the scene into the most
glorious light.

CHAPTER ELEVEN

SYMBOL AND HISTORY

St. John's Gospel ends with the miraculous catch of 153 fishes. The Risen Christ appears to seven disciples who have dropped their spiritual vocation of fishing for men, and returned to their secular work of fishing for fish. Accordingly, in language strongly reminiscent of the original Call of the Fishermen at Luke 5:1–11, Jesus recalls them to their spiritual task. This is symbolized by the number 153, supposed to be the number of species of fish in the whole world. In short, John is saying in pictorial language exactly what St. Matthew, the straight man among the evangelists, says in plain language at the end of his gospel: 'Go ye therefore and make disciples of all the nations.'

We have already seen how John translates Mark's symbols, the ass's colt, and the temple made without hands, into plainer speech for a wider readership. Here we see the opposite process. John wraps up in mysterious symbol a truth which Matthew expressed plainly and directly. Perhaps John is telling his readers that 'interpretations belong to God' (Genesis 40:8), and that the Church alone has the right to interpret the mysteries of the Kingdom of God. Mysterious language invites thought and prayer and consultation. It is less immediately available.

In view of this two-way traffic, the unwrapping and re-wrapping of the gospels' message, we can no longer trace a straight line of development from Mark, the earliest gospel, as though it were also the most primitive, through Matthew and Luke, up to John, the latest and most sophisticated. Mark is by no means the least sophisticated. Nor can we assume that what is presented in symbols is in any way less 'historical' than what is told directly. To argue that because a story means a lot it probably didn't happen would be a gross non sequitur. We have no rational grounds for doubting the historicity of either the sign, such as the catch of 153 fishes, or the thing signified, the commission of the disciples by the Risen Christ. Mark's symbols, such as the Ass's Colt, the Withered Fig Tree, the Rent Veil of the Temple, could well have been historic in the sense that they were the actual means by which the eyes of St. Peter, whom St. Mark interpreted, were opened to the truth. If St. Mark's readers had asked him: 'Did someone actually see the temple veil rent from the top, or is this just a parable to declare the meaning of the Passion?', St. Mark might well have answered: 'Your question is hardly relevant to my purpose, which is to give you the gospel. The truth which makes you free can be conveyed equally well by history or by parable. You might as well ask me whether I actually saw the farmer cast his seed on three bad soils and three good soils, or the lamp hidden under a bushel measure. Please notice that I have coupled the Rending of the Veil with the Centurion's Confession, and placed both together immediately after the full price of our ransom has been paid. If you follow my clues you can understand the meaning of the events which most surely took place in Jerusalem a generation ago. And thereby you will also understand the seemingly tragic events taking place in Rome now. What is more, you will understand the lengths to which the Son of God went in search of your own soul, and be enabled to love him with all your heart and mind and strength and enter his kingdom. From inside the kingdom all will be clear. "Whoever has the will to do the will of God shall know".[25]

Mark's Gospel assumes that both he and his readers accept as historic the facts of Jesus' life and Passion and Resurrection. In fact they were written down centuries before, in all essentials, in the Law and the Prophets and the Psalms. The sole purpose of Mark's Gospel therefore is to reveal the meaning of events whose historicity was never in doubt. This he does by powerful symbols, by frequent scriptural allusions, and by careful arranging and editing of his stories. Fourteen of his stories are dovetailed to give emphasis or to assist interpretation. All the stories are placed in their right context in his unfolding drama of revelation and response. Thus the second and lesser multitude feeding has a special significance in its context, signifying the intensity of our Saviour's struggle with our blindness. The Disobedient Leper has a special meaning at the head of the conflict complex, indicating the danger of undisciplined enthusiasm in a time of persecution. Each incident on the journey to Jerusalem, and in Jerusalem itself, is given heightened significance by its context.

When Mark calls his book a Gospel, he means that it is a signpost to the Kingdom of God, which he equates with eternal life. Compare Mark 9:43 and Mark 9:45: 'It is better for thee to enter into life . . .' with Mark 9:47: 'It is better for thee to enter into the Kingdom of God . . .'.

There are two ways of verifying a signpost, the academic and the practical. The academic way is to join the circle sitting round the post, endlessly scraping off layers of paint and arguing whether the wood beneath, could it be reached, is the pine of parable or the oak of

25 John 7:17 (New English Bible).

history. The practical way is to pick up one's pack and march boldly forward where the signpost points. Christians in Mark's day demonstrated the truth of his Gospel by their willingness to follow through death and beyond, and their successors in every generation since have added their testimony.

Appendix 1

ST. MARK'S PRIORITY

When the synoptic gospels give three accounts of the same incident, a clear line of development can be seen among them. The accounts progress from a looser to a more exact grammar; from a verbose and conversational style to a succinct and literary style; from a less accurate to a more accurate nomenclature.

Each line of development points clearly to Mark's priority. So does the retention in Mark of words in the original Aramaic vernacular which are omitted in Matthew and Luke. It is easy to see why Matthew and Luke substitute 'Herod the Tetrarch' for Mark's less exact 'Herod the King'; and give 'on the third day' for Mark's 'after three days'; and omit Mark's 'in the days of Abiathar the High Priest', when in fact the high priest was Ahimelech. It is not easy to see why Mark should amend the other evangelists by deliberately adding pleonasms and inexactitudes.

Again, in nine of the stories which appear in both Matthew and Mark, the miraculous element is distinctly enhanced in Matthew's version.

(1) Matthew gives two demoniacs in Decapolis to Mark's one.

(2) In Mark Jairus pleads with Jesus that his daughter is at the point of death; in Matthew that she is dead already.

(3) In Matthew Peter walks on the water as well as Jesus.

(4) Matthew gives two blind men at Jericho to Mark's one.

(5) In Mark the cursed fig tree is found withered next day; in Matthew it withers instantly.

(6) Matthew adds to the darkness at the crucifixion an earthquake and rent rocks. (And an earthquake at the Resurrection also.)

(7) Matthew adds to the Resurrection of Jesus, a Resurrection of saints.

(8) and (9) The figures for the two multitude feedings, 5,000 and 4,000, evidently became fixed when made the basis of subsequent teaching by Jesus (Mark 8:19–21). They do not vary in any of the gospels. Matthew seems to have hit upon a very clever device for doubling the numbers whilst retaining the figures. He writes 'Five thousand men beside women and children' at Matthew 14:21, and 'Four thousand men beside women and children' at Matthew 15:38. Both these expanding phrases are peculiar to Matthew.

It is easy to see why Matthew should enhance the glory of God by nine times enhancing Mark's miracles. We see the same process at work in the development of some Old Testament stories. It is inconceivable that Mark should wish to detract from the glory of God by diminishing Matthew.

Luke records six of these nine stories. In every case he follows Mark's version exactly, and ignores all Matthew's improvements, indicating his dependence on Mark's versions, and his ignorance of Matthew's versions.

If we contend that Mark is a late attempt to conflate Matthew and Luke by following first one and then the other, we multiply one absurdity into three. First, why should Luke diminish the glory of God in six of Matthew's stories? Second, why should Mark dinimish the glory of God in the three stories which do not appear in Luke, that is, the Walking on the Water, the Four Thousand, and the Withered Fig Tree? Third, why should Mark, when faced with two versions of the other six stories, choose the diminished version in all six cases?

So long as Mark was regarded as 'seemingly incoherent', lacking in both biographical and theological articulation', as chaotic as 'unstrung beads', it was just possible to squeeze his supposedly amorphous mass into second or third place among the evangelists. But only if Mark had 'no chronology of his own', apart from what he derived from his alleged sources, Matthew and Luke.[26] Once it has been demonstrated that Mark does have a chronology, an intelligent and purposeful structure, his priority is assured. Mark cannot be an unintelligent copier of other documents if he uses dovetailing, symbolism, irony, play upon titles, and other devices, to signal a gospel message to a beleaguered church. The gospels are like children's building bricks which can be fitted into their box in any order you please, until you discover that there is a picture on the bricks. Then only one order is possible, the order that shows the picture.

Mark pictures a drama of revelation and response, a desperate struggle of incarnate divine truth with the blindness of corrupt humanity. The drama culminates in two decisive victories for the truth, Peter's confession at 8:29, and the centurion's confession at 15:39.

But it was not possible for Matthew and Luke to follow this structure all the way for two good reasons. First, because both Matthew and Luke added birth stories in which the true identity of Jesus of Nazareth was revealed to others before Peter. Secondly, because both Matthew and Luke had so much material to add, from 'Q' and other sources. This material was of such infinite value to the

---

26 W.R. Farmer: 'Modern developments of the Griesbach Hypothesis' *New Testament Studies* Vol.23 1977, 275–295.

Church that it could not be omitted. Nor could it be added without swamping Mark's strict structure.

Luke, with his literary skills, makes a geographical piston movement in two volumes. In Volume 1, the Gospel, the action begins at Nazareth, and spreads through all Galilee and beyond, culminating in Jerusalem. In Volume 2, the Acts, the action begins in Jerusalem where the first volume ended, spreads out through all Syria and the Roman world, culminating in Rome. So St. Luke places the Rejection at Nazareth right at the beginning of the ministry, before the specimen day in Capernaum, and the Call of the Fishermen. He openly declares that this is a literary and not a chronological construction when he locates at the outset of the Ministry the words spoken at Nazareth, 'Whatsoever we have heard done in Capernaum, do also here in thy country' (Luke 4:23). Similarly Luke emphasizes the new beginning from Jerusalem by making no mention of any Resurrection appearances in Galilee, even though these are given in both Matthew and John, and promised in Mark. Mark 16:7 ('Tell his disciples and Peter that he goeth before you into Galilee') becomes Luke 24:6: '. . . Remember how he spake unto you when he was yet in Galilee.'

Matthew, the scribe instructed in the Kingdom of Heaven, marshalls his material into nine great teaching sections. Accordingly he begins his account of the ministry with the greatest of these, Matthew 5–7, the Sermon on the Mount, the Law of God interpreted by the Christ of God. Then this longest of the teaching sections is followed by the longest of his miracle sections, Matthew 8:1–9:35, vindicating and illustrating the teaching.

So it comes about that the three synoptists have three different ways of beginning the story of Jesus' ministry. Matthew's didactic arrangement, Mark's evangelical arrangement, and Luke's geographical arrangement necessitate three different sequences of the same events.

The stories of Mark 1:16 to 6:6 come in for considerable re-arrangement in Matthew and Luke. But thereafter Matthew and Luke both follow Mark's structure throughout. In the run up to Peter's confession, then the journey to Jerusalem, then the Jerusalem conflict, then the 'Little Apocalypse', then the Passion, they adhere to Mark's sequence, each making his own additions and omissions but not altering Mark's order.

Matthew's structure and Luke's both flow from Mark's as naturally as water flows down hill. If the Church emerged from the holocaust of the Neronian persecution, Jewish war, and slaughter of the apostles with one brief gospel, coming from the interpreter of the chief apostle, but stopping short of Resurrection appearances, it was natural that the churches should undertake to fill out and finish Mark's work. Evidently the Syrian and Roman ends of the church undertook this work independently, giving us the two distinctive Gospels of Matthew and Luke. It was natural that Luke should omit Mark 6: 45–8:26, for this is Mark's 'second touch' passage, and deliberately repetitive. It was natural that Matthew, who includes much more of Mark, all but fifty-five verses in fact, should include the 'second touch' passage also, apart from the last two healings therein, the Deaf Mute of Decapolis and the Blind Man of Bethsaida. For these are the two healings most strictly concealed and most laboriously performed, indicating the agony of Jesus' struggle to open his disciples' eyes. These two healings therefore would have least appeal to Matthew, with his love of the miraculous.

But trying to make the synoptic Gospels flow the other way, and make Mark last, is like trying to make the waters flow up hill. Mark is basic. His structure alone covers his whole book and gives meaning to everything in it. Matthew and Luke are derivative. They both follow Mark most of the way, and when they substitute structures of their own, they differ from each other.

Matthew and Luke only agree with each other struc-
turally when both agree with Mark. Neither Matthew
nor Luke were in any position to reproduce all the rich
irony and high drama which Mark derived from his
single-minded concentration on the Passion theme. Yet
both Matthew and Luke show clear editorial skills of their
own when they handle material not derived from Mark.

Dr. J. Alexander Findlay has pointed out Matthew's
skilful use of the Greek word *hetairos*, 'comrade', which
occurs only three times in the New Testament, and all
three in Matthew's Gospel. Jesus addresses Judas as
hetairos when Judas betrays him with a kiss, and the
same word occurs in two parables peculiar to Matthew.
In both parables the word is addressed to a comrade in
the act of breaking comradeship. The disgruntled vineyard worker at Matthew 19:13 is challenged: 'Comrade, I
do thee no wrong . . . is thine eye envious because I am
generous?' And the man attending a wedding feast who
failed to put on a wedding garment is addressed in the
same way (Matthew 23:12). These two parables gain
enormously in value if we follow Matthew's hints that
Jesus is pleading for the soul of his breakaway disciple,
Judas Iscariot.[27]

Some of Luke's non-Markan material is added very
naturally to Markan stories, such as the Rejection at
Nazareth and the Call of the Fishermen, which Luke
expands. The rest is inserted at the beginning and end,
and in two large blocks, one in Galilee, (Luke 6:20–8:3),
and the other on the journey to Jerusalem (Luke 9:51–
18:14). But into these two blocks Luke has inserted three
pericopes from Mark. He removes these three stories
from their Markan context, and gives them fresh and
fuller treatment. These three pericopes therefore tell us
much about St. Luke's editorial policy.

27 J. Alexander Findlay: *Jesus and his Parables* (London 1950),
especially 56–58.

First, the Beelzebub controversy is removed from its Markan position as climax of the Galilean conflict stories. It is thereby set free from Mark's complicated theme of the disobedient leper, and from its dovetail with the opposition of Jesus' kindred, and greatly simplified. Instead it is placed in chapter eleven, where it forms an introduction to the denunciation of 'this evil generation', and the woes to the Pharisees and lawyers. It is also given fuller treatment, being preceded by the exorcism of a dumb devil, and followed by the parable of the Empty Heart (Luke 11:24–26).

Second, the story of the Anointing at Bethany is removed from Mark's Passion narrative, and instead a very different anointing story is inserted in Galilee (Luke 7:36–50). Again Luke simplifies and amplifies. Luke avoids the complicated symbolism and bitter irony of Mark's Passion pericopes, and gives instead a straight-forward story with a clear Gospel message. The woman who was a sinner and the Pharisee who criticized her fulfil the same roles as the younger and elder brothers in the parable of the Prodigal Son.

Third, the pericope of the Two Great Commandments is removed from its setting in Mark's Jerusalem conflict stories, (Mark 12:28–34), and placed in the Great Insertion at Luke 10:25–42, where Luke has space to add a full exposition. The second great commandment is first explained by the parable of the Good Samaritan. Then the necessary priority of the first commandment is made clear by the story of the two sisters, Martha and Mary. Luke shows why the love of neighbour is essential, and why it fails unless the love of God comes before it. The three stories of the Lawyer's Question, the Good Samaritan, and the Two Sisters belong together as surely as the three parables of redemption, the Lost Sheep, the Lost Coin, and the Lost Sons, belong together in Luke 15.

Mark wrote for the Church. His Gospel is a handbook for Christian prophets and teachers, experts in interpret-

ing the words and works of Jesus to the people to whom it
was given to know the mystery of the Kingdom of God.
But Luke has in mind 'Your Excellency Theophilus', the
honest inquirer. Therefore he unwraps some of Mark's
mysteries when he re-positions and explains the three
pericopes of the Beelzebub Controversy, the Anointing,
and the Two Great Commandments.

Matthew's constructions and Luke's are totally diverse
when they do not follow Mark's. So are their birth stories,
genealogies, and Resurrection stories. When they come
to deal with Mark's stark Passion story, Matthew makes
four additions and Luke five. Matthew inserts the
Remorse of Judas, the Dream of Pilate's Wife, the extra
portents at Calvary, and the story of the Chief Priests'
Guard. Luke inserts the Trial before Herod, the Lament
of Jerusalem's Daughters, the Penitent Thief, and Jesus'
prayers, 'Father forgive them . . .', and 'Father into Thy
hands I commend my spirit'. All Luke's five insertions
are different from Matthew's four. When Matthew and
Luke do make the same amendment to Mark, for
example when they both insert an exorcism before the
Beelzebub Controversy, and healings before the Feeding
of the Five Thousand, they do so in entirely different
language. There is only one solution to all this which will
stand up to examination, that Matthew and Luke wrote
in full dependence on the text of Mark 1:1–16:8, and in
full independence of each other. Both the Syrian and
Roman ends of the Church recognized the need to
incorporate Mark's brief and truncated account in a
fuller and completed Gospel. In effect this provides Mark
with two independent commentators who knew his
circumstances far better than we do. We no longer have
any excuse for failing to understand Mark's special
genius as a Gospel maker. Let the lion free.

Appendix 2

AN OUTLINE OF ST. MARK'S STRUCTURE

1:1–20
Prologue, showing how Jesus' ministry was begun.

1:21–39
Specimen Day, showing how Jesus' ministry was conducted.

1:40–3:35
How opposition arose.

4:1–34
How Jesus enunciated his teaching — the judging parables.

4:35–5:43
How Jesus validated his teaching — four specimen miracles.

6:1–48 *The Judgement Falls.*
The rejection at Nazareth and the murder of the Baptist indicate Galilee's self-rejection. The mission of the Twelve indicates how the New Israel will be formed. Therefore the great Messianic Banquet is given, the multitude are bidden farewell, and a final sign is given to the Twelve alone, the Walking on the Waters.

6:49–8:30 *The Galilean Agony.*
The Twelve panic. They had not understood about the loaves because their hearts were hardened. The formation of the New Israel cannot yet go forward. God's saving plan can be redeemed only by a return to all the trials of the Galilean ministry, and a re-enactment of all the signs of Christhood, leading to a second Messianic Banquet. The contraction of this second banquet, and the greater labour and greater secrecy of the healing miracles, indicate the intensity of Jesus' struggle with the disciples' blindness. Then a sign is categorically refused, and Jesus pleads passionately with the Twelve to understand the signs already given. Jesus' hard-won victory is then shown by the arrival at Bethsaida, the healing of a blind man by a second touch, and Peter's confession in answer to a second question.

8:31–10:45 *The Road to Jerusalem.*
8:31–38 The first prediction of the Passion and Resurrection is followed by Peter's failure to understand, and Jesus' call to both disciples and multitude to take up the cross.

9:1–29
Three interim episodes between the first and second predictions. 9:1–8 shows the sublimity of Jesus' new calling, surpassing even the Law and the Prophets. 9:9–13 shows the price he must pay, foreshadowed by the fate of his fore-runner. 9:14–29 shows the splendour of the mountain vision worked out in the valley of our need.

9:30–50
The second prediction is likewise followed by failure among the Twelve, which is corrected by teaching on the glory and the cost of discipleship.

10:1–31
Three interim episodes between the second and third

predictions, showing the nature of the kingdom which
Jesus brings, and why Judea will reject it.

10:32–45
The third prediction is again followed by disciple-failure,
which again gives rise to dominical teaching on the *via
crucis*.

10:46–12:44 *The Jerusalem Conflict.*
A second healing of the blind introduces a partial
opening of the eyes of the crowd when nigh to the city.
This enables Jesus to exercise messianic authority in the
temple, leading to direct confrontation with the authorities. In all the verbal battles which follow, Jesus is
completely victorious, and the section ends with Jesus
sitting in the purified temple as judge.

13:1–37 *Looking Ahead.*
Before his Passion, which must now follow, Jesus warns
his closest disciples of the Passion which must be theirs
under Nero, and tells them how to meet it.

14:1–15:49 *The Significance of the Passion.*
Here the use of structure to show the true meaning of
what is happening reaches its climax. The careful notices
of time at each of the three-hourly watches, and frequent
allusions to the fulfilment of scriptural prophecy, show
the sovereign rule of Almighty God over all that
happens. The bitter ironies of the anointing beforehand
for burial, the mis-heard call for Elijah, the two false
accusations at the two trials, with their self-fulfilling
prophecies, and the mockeries, do more than enhance the
drama. They also assist the observant interpreter. The
opening of the Holy of Holies and the first Gentile
confession when Jesus dies show just what his death has
achieved for us.

15:40–16:8 *Prelude to the Resurrection.*